AF256019

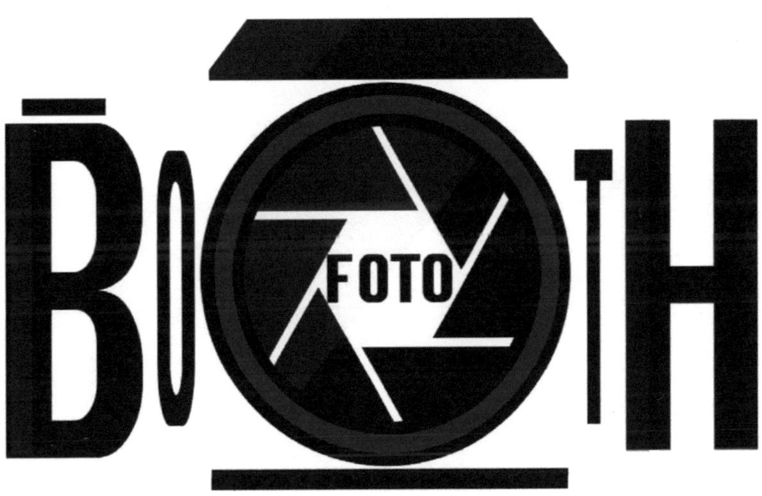
B
FOTO
OTH

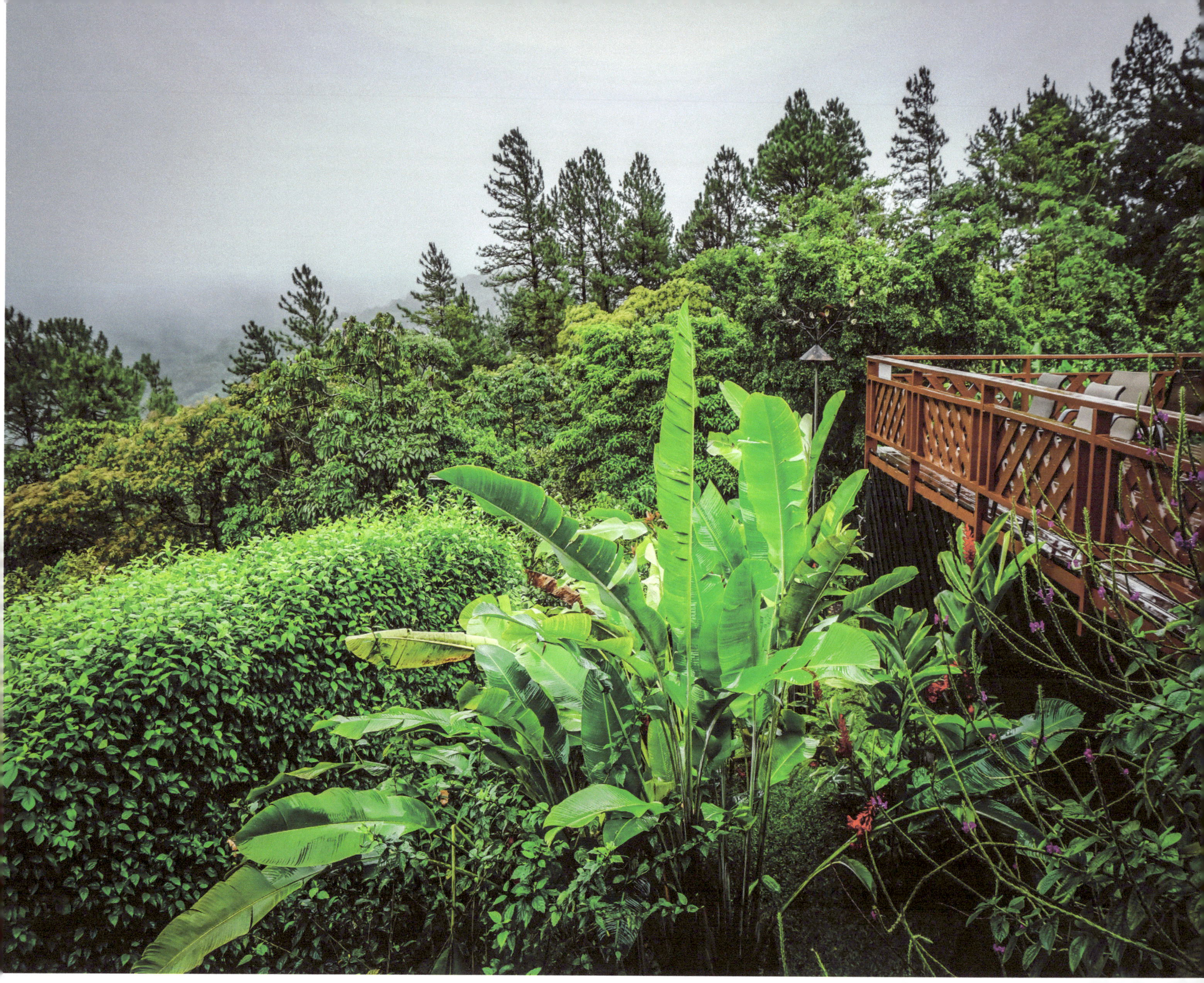

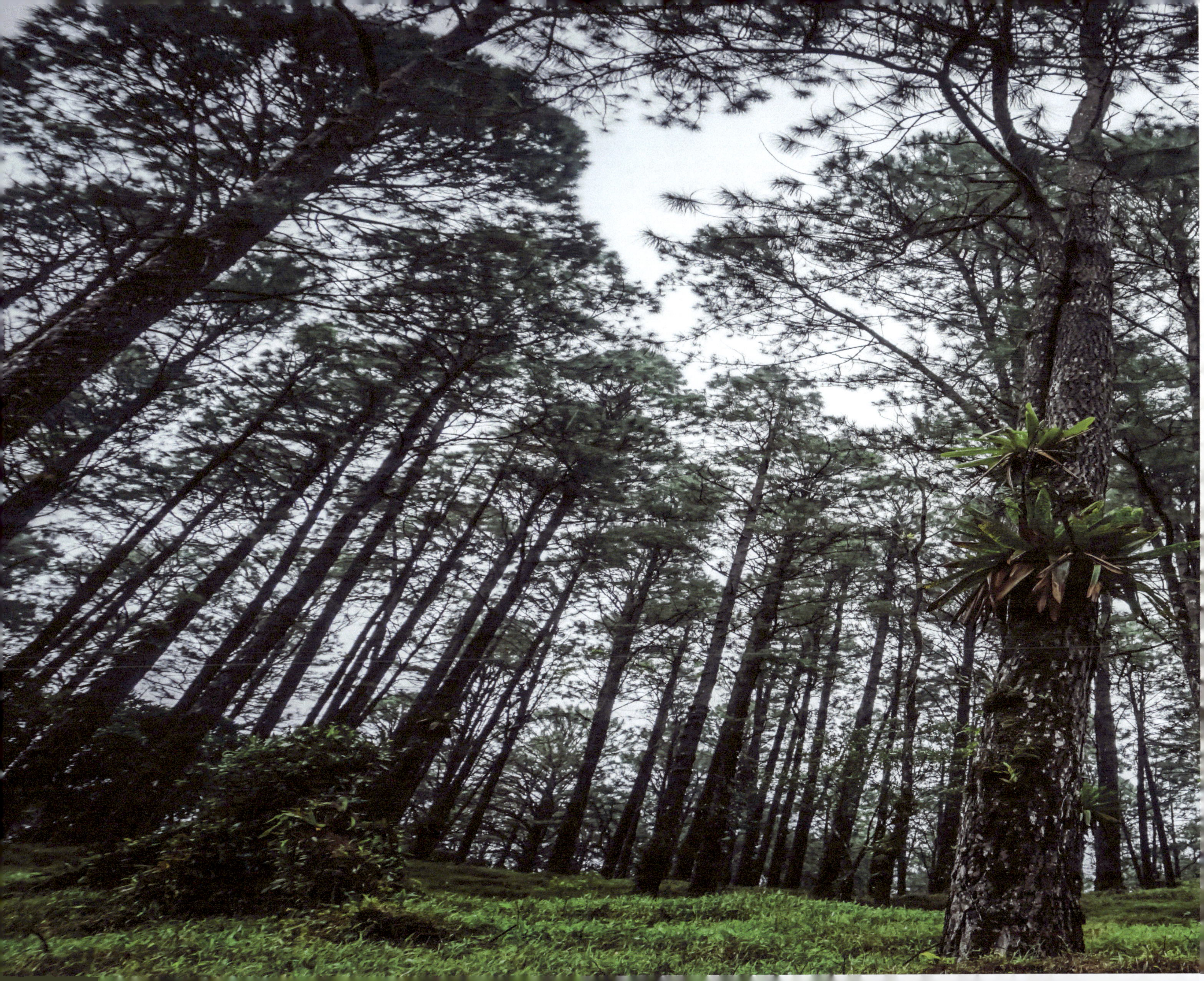

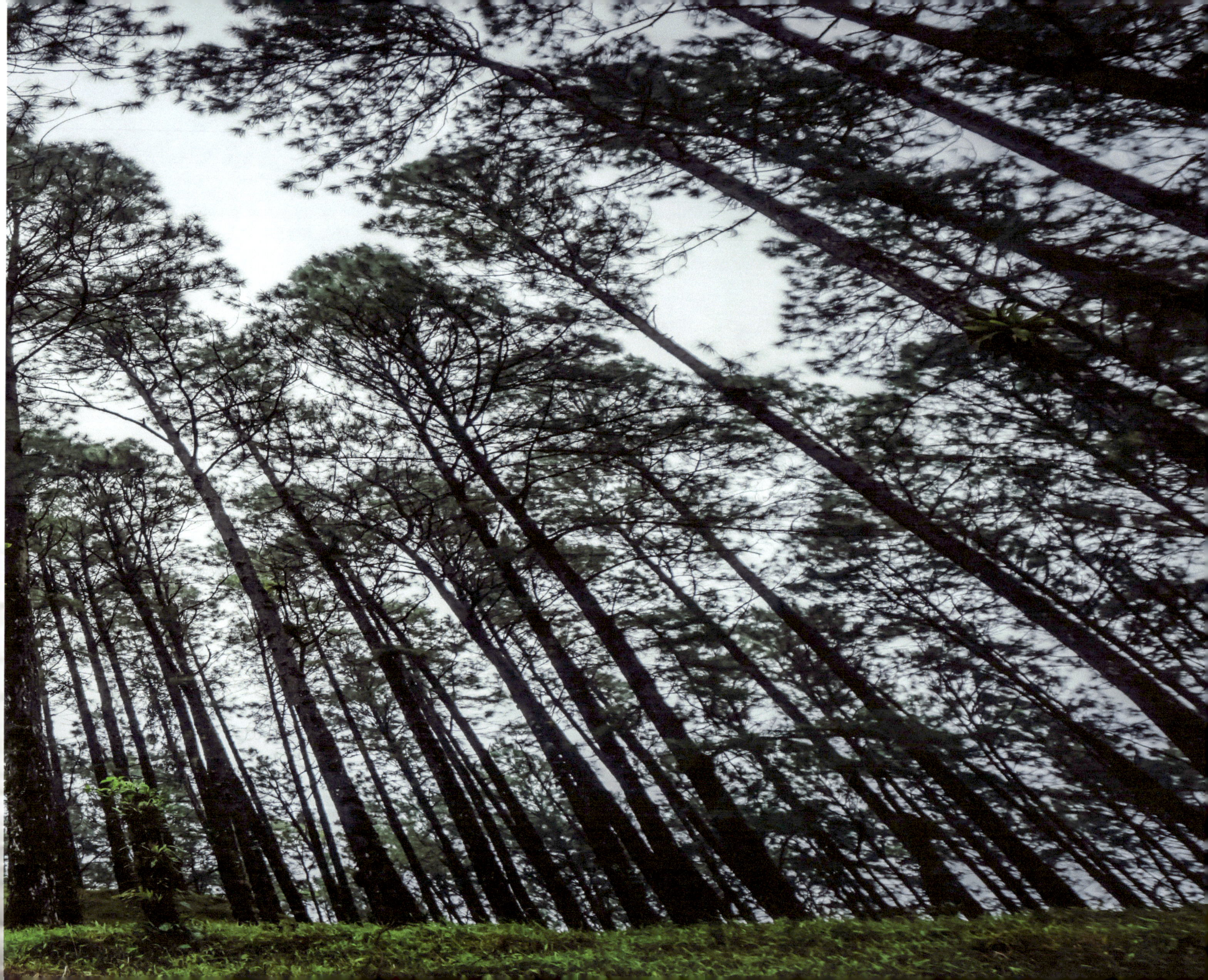

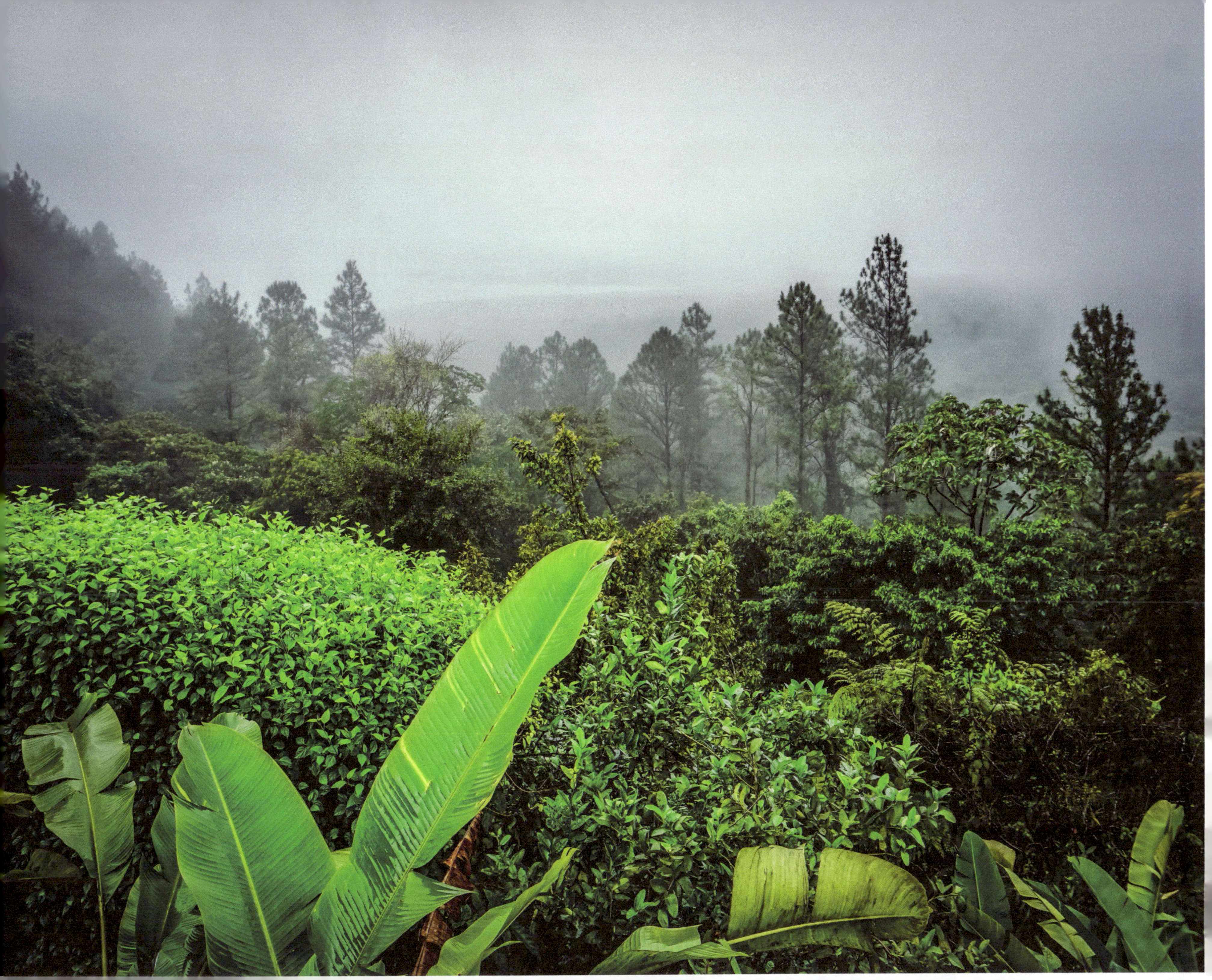

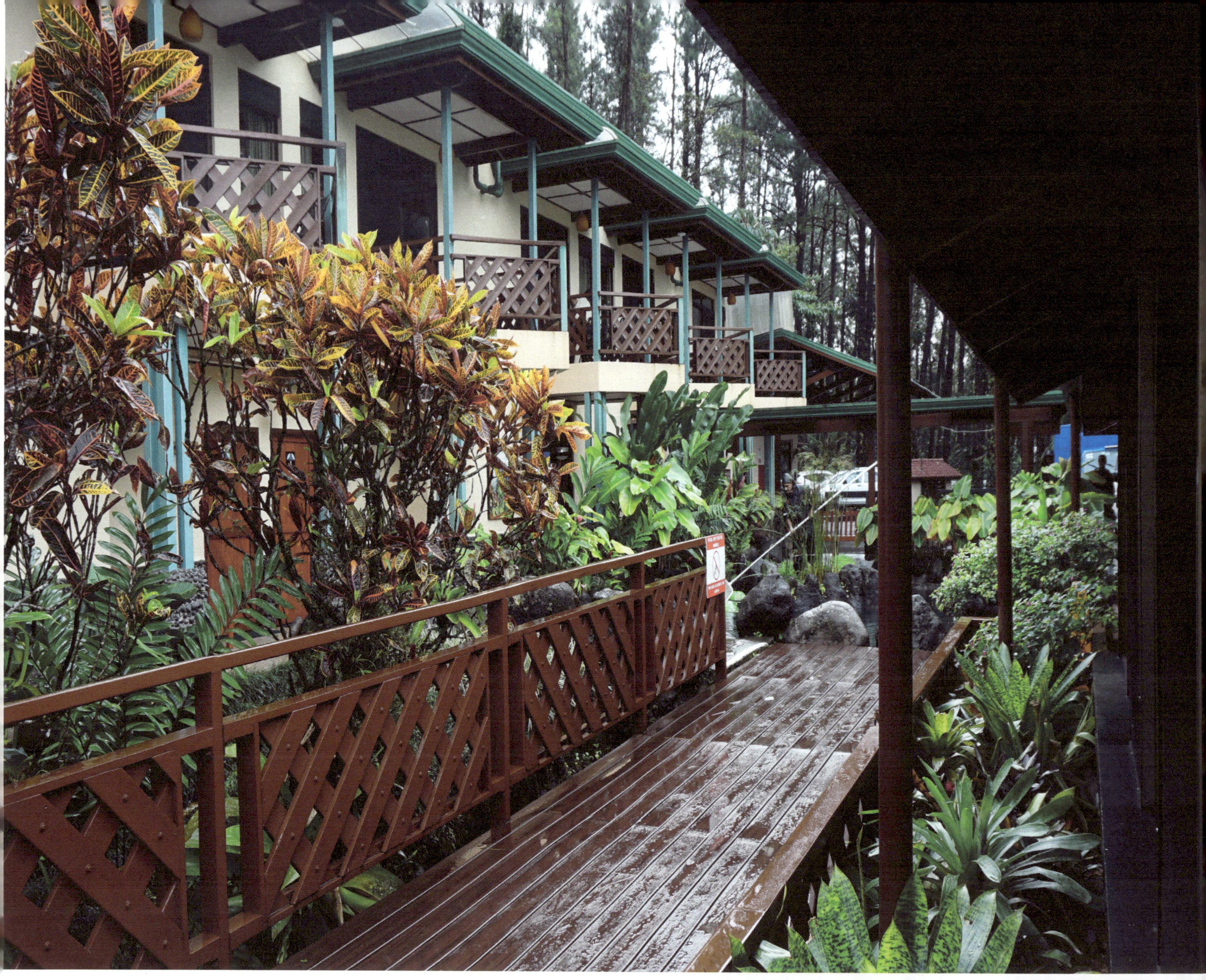

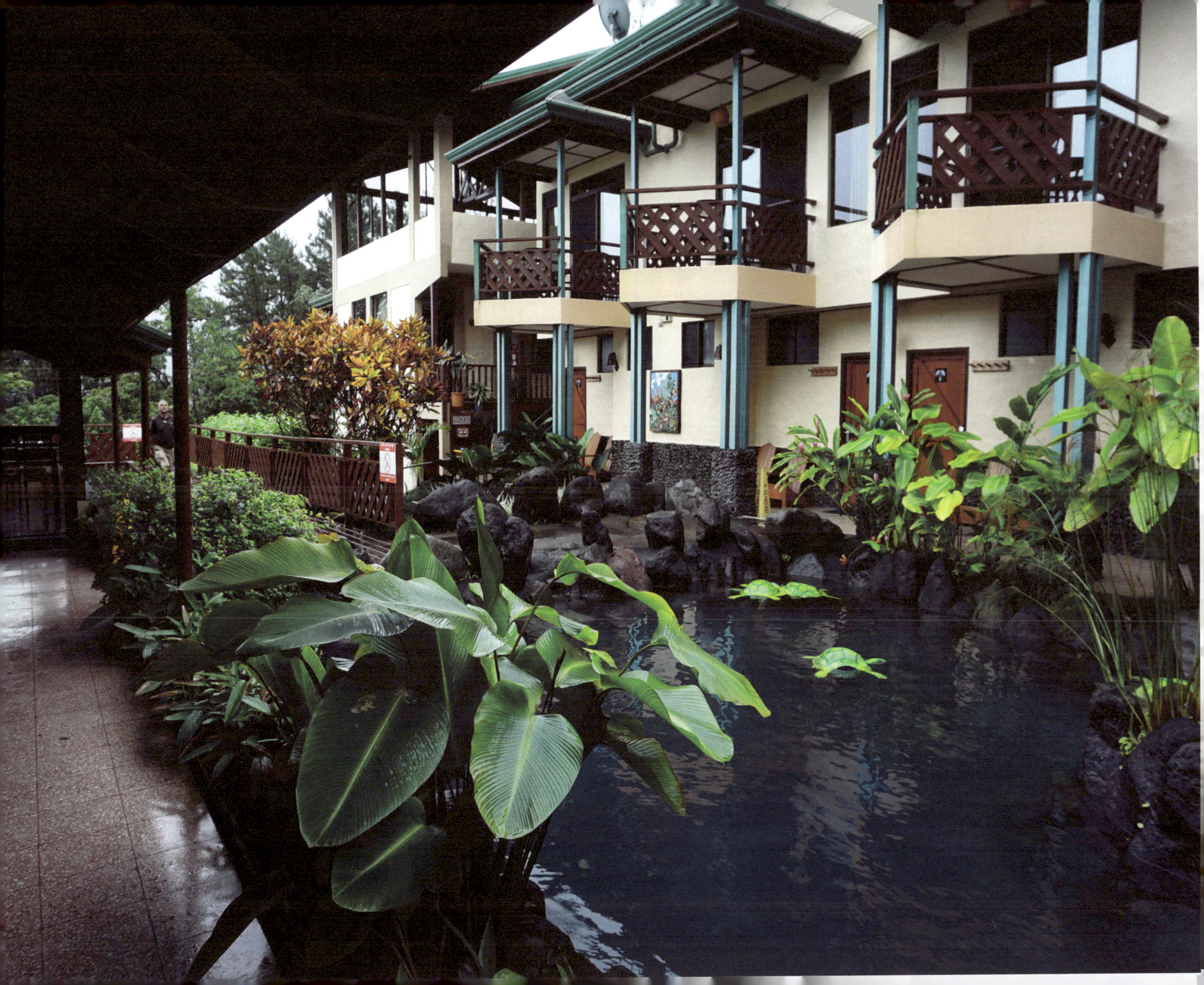

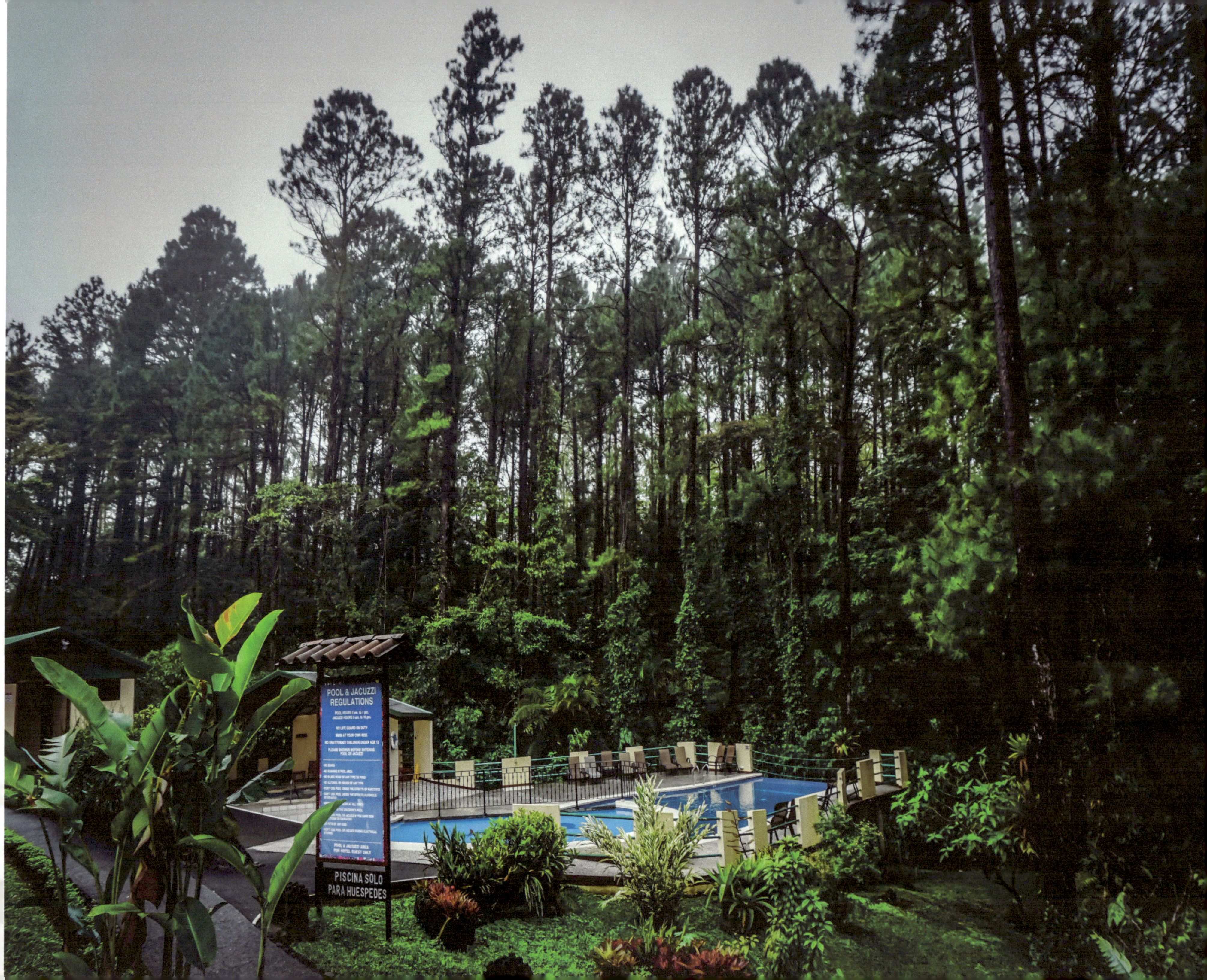
POOL & JACUZZI
REGULATIONS
NO LIFE GUARD ON DUTY
SWIM AT YOUR OWN RISK
PLEASE SHOWER BEFORE ENTERING
POOL & JACUZZI AREA
FOR HOTEL GUEST ONLY
PISCINA SOLO
PARA HUESPEDES

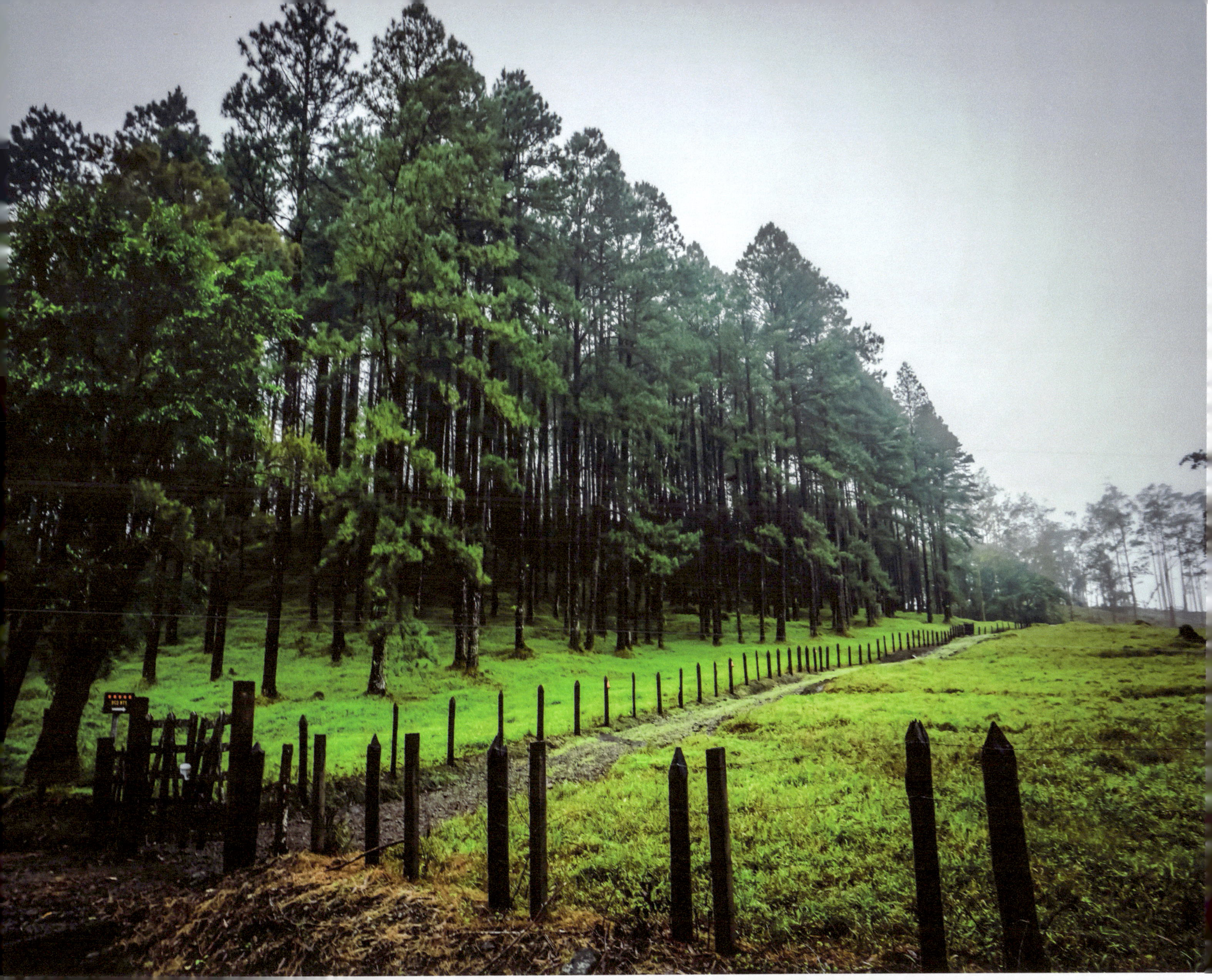

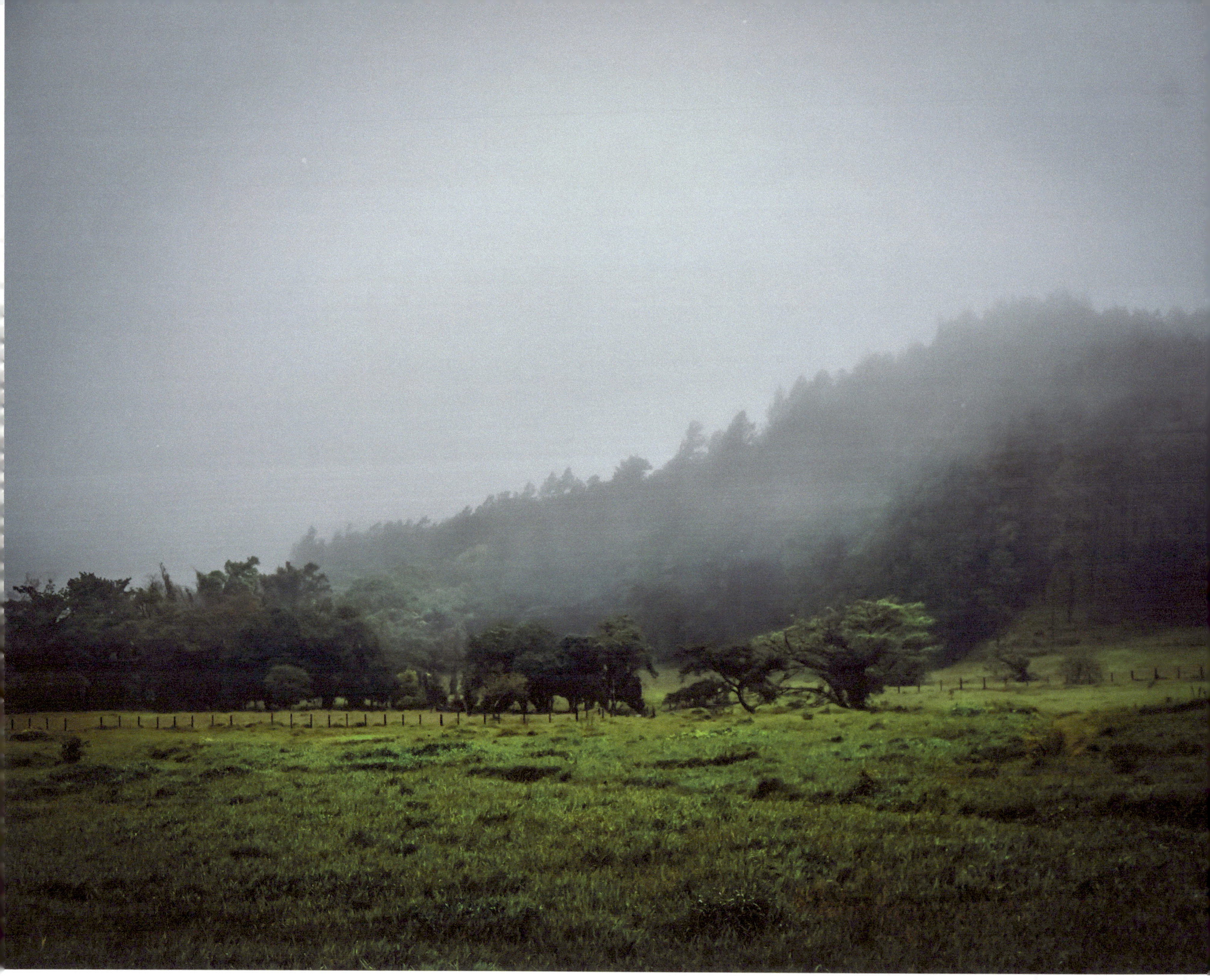

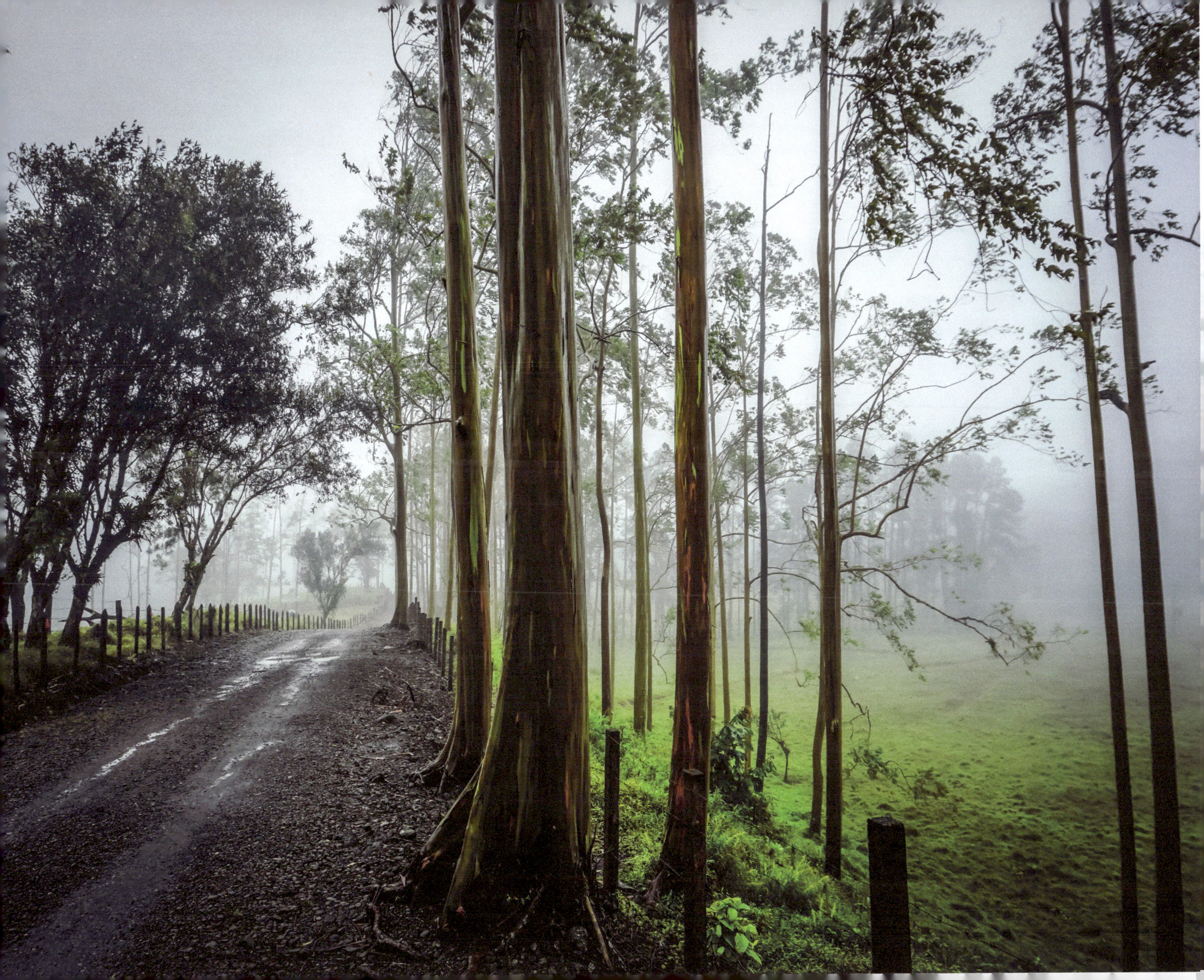

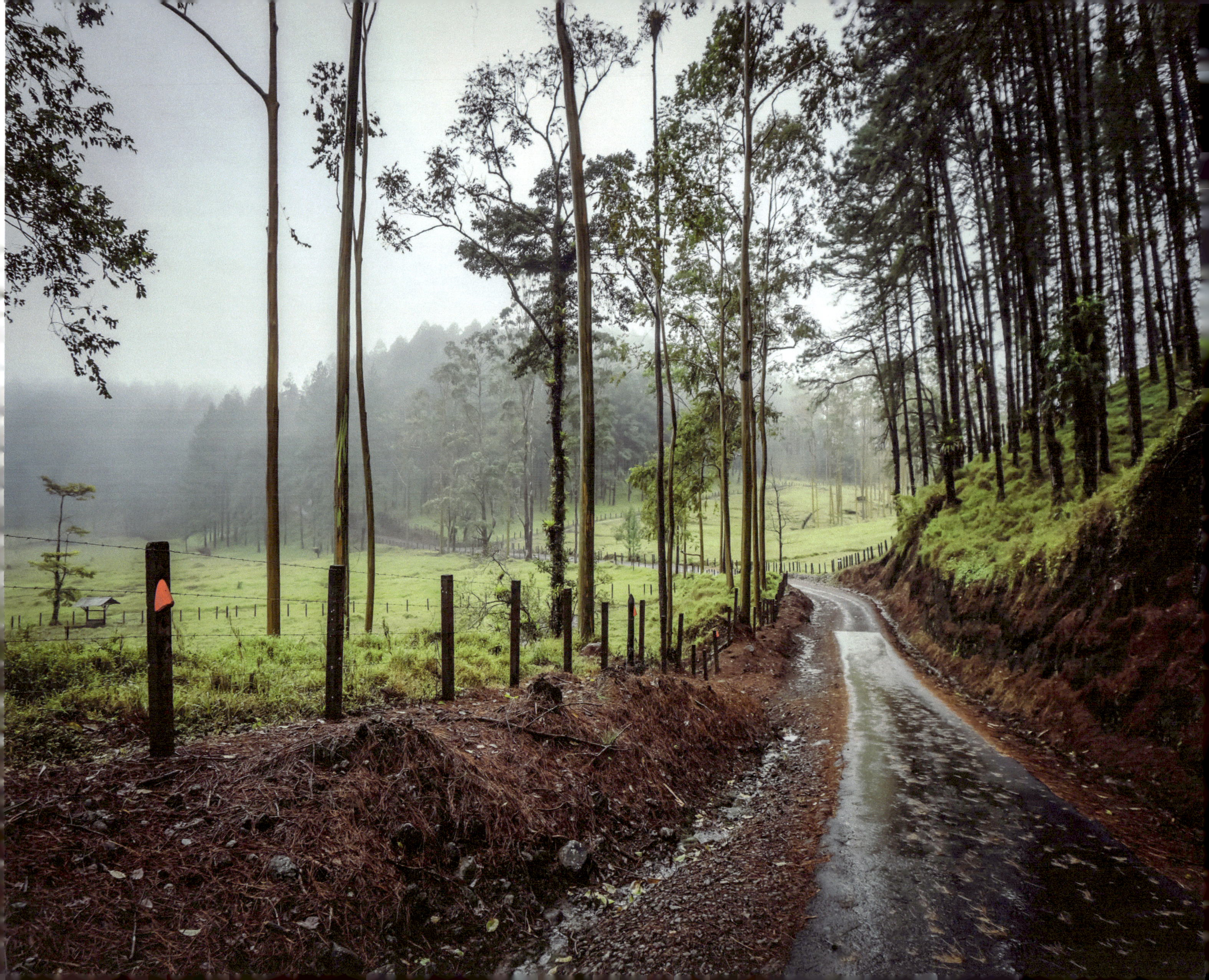

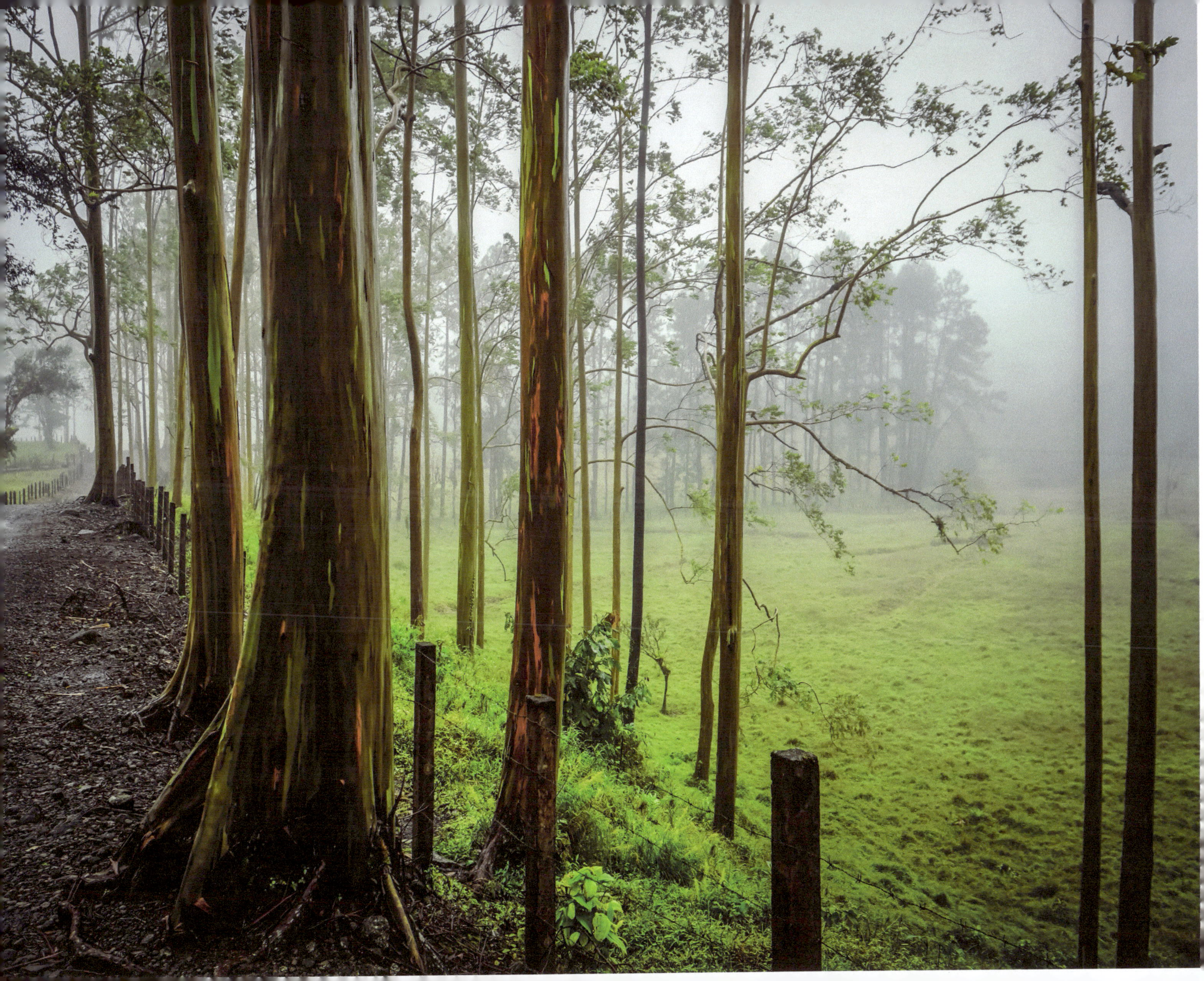

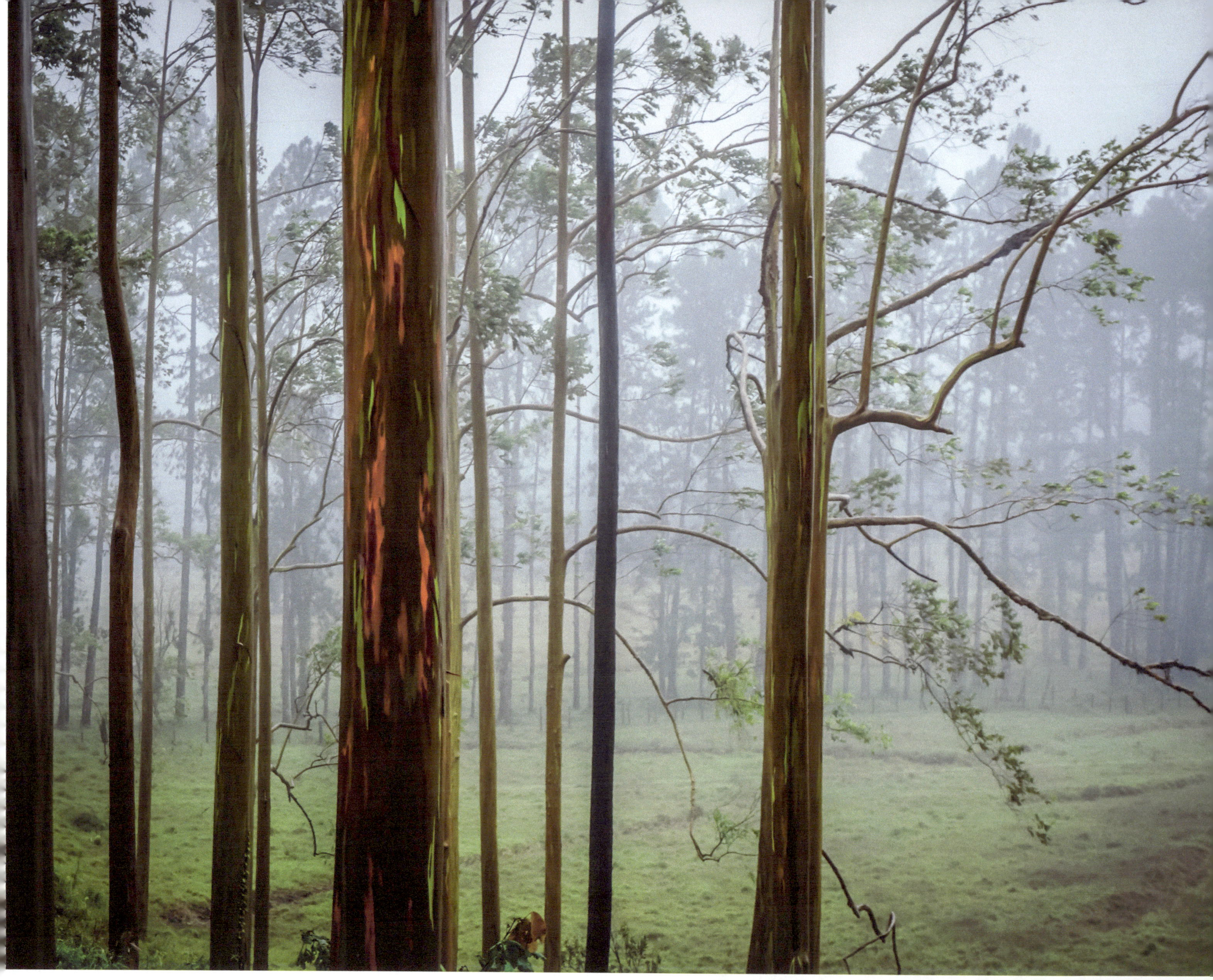

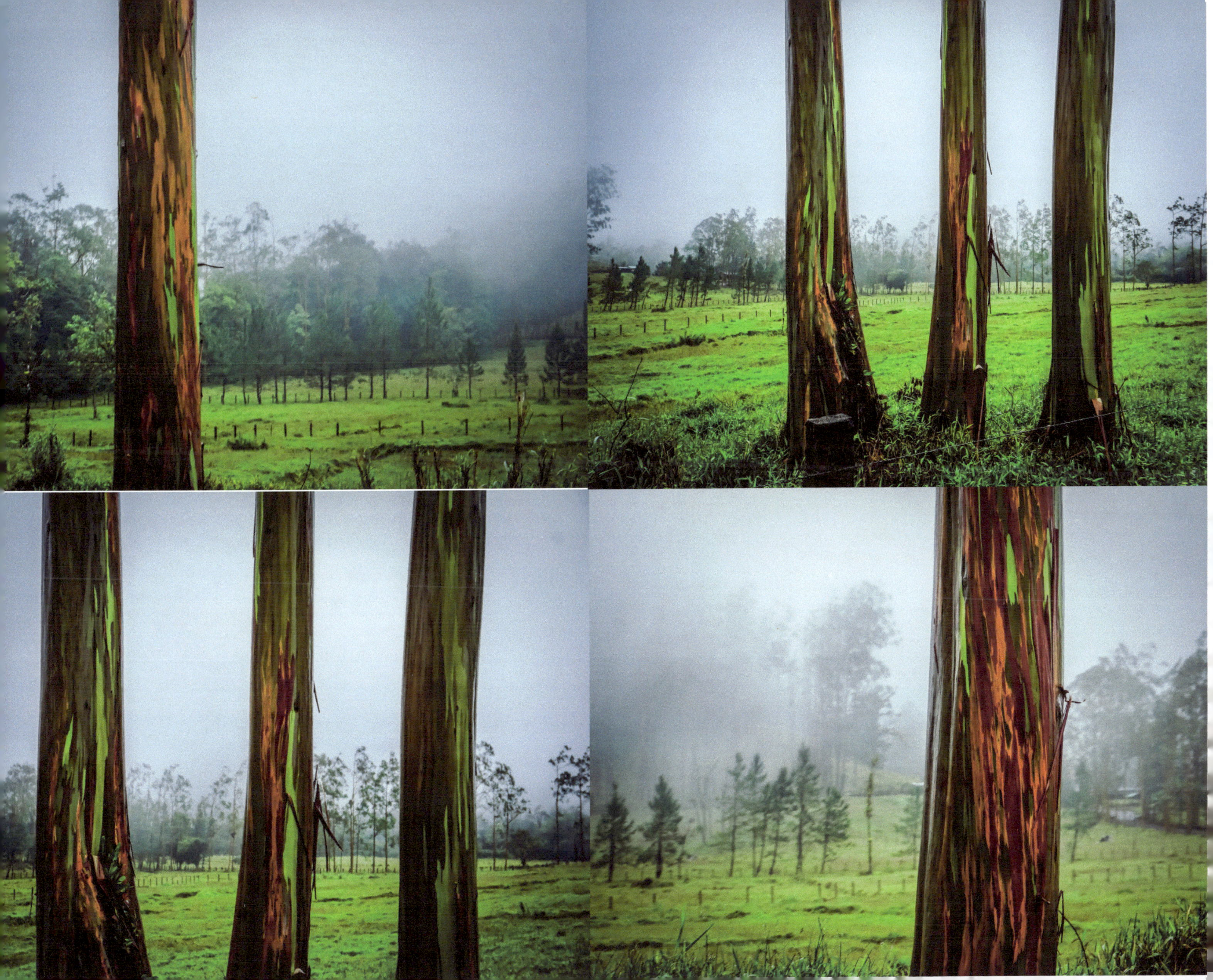

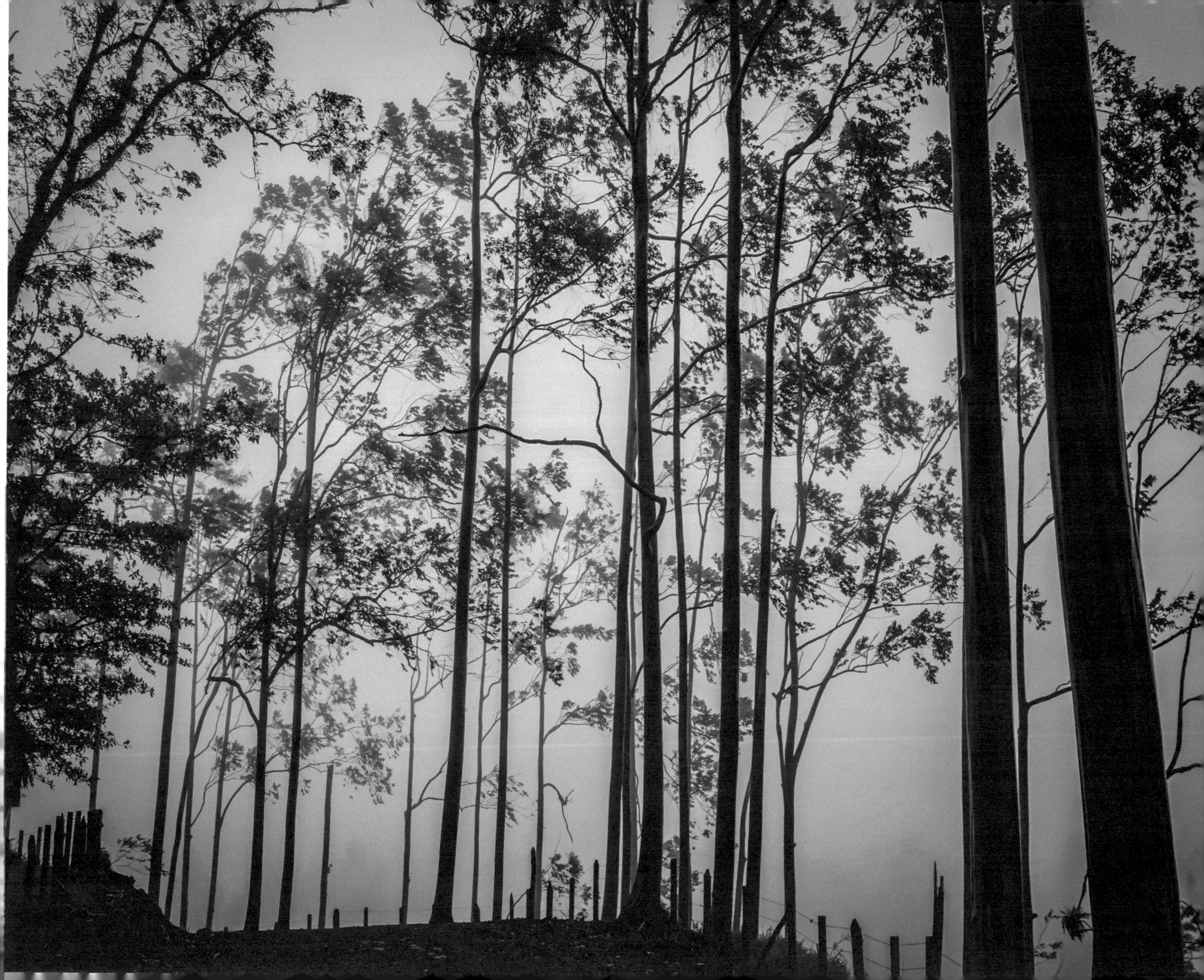

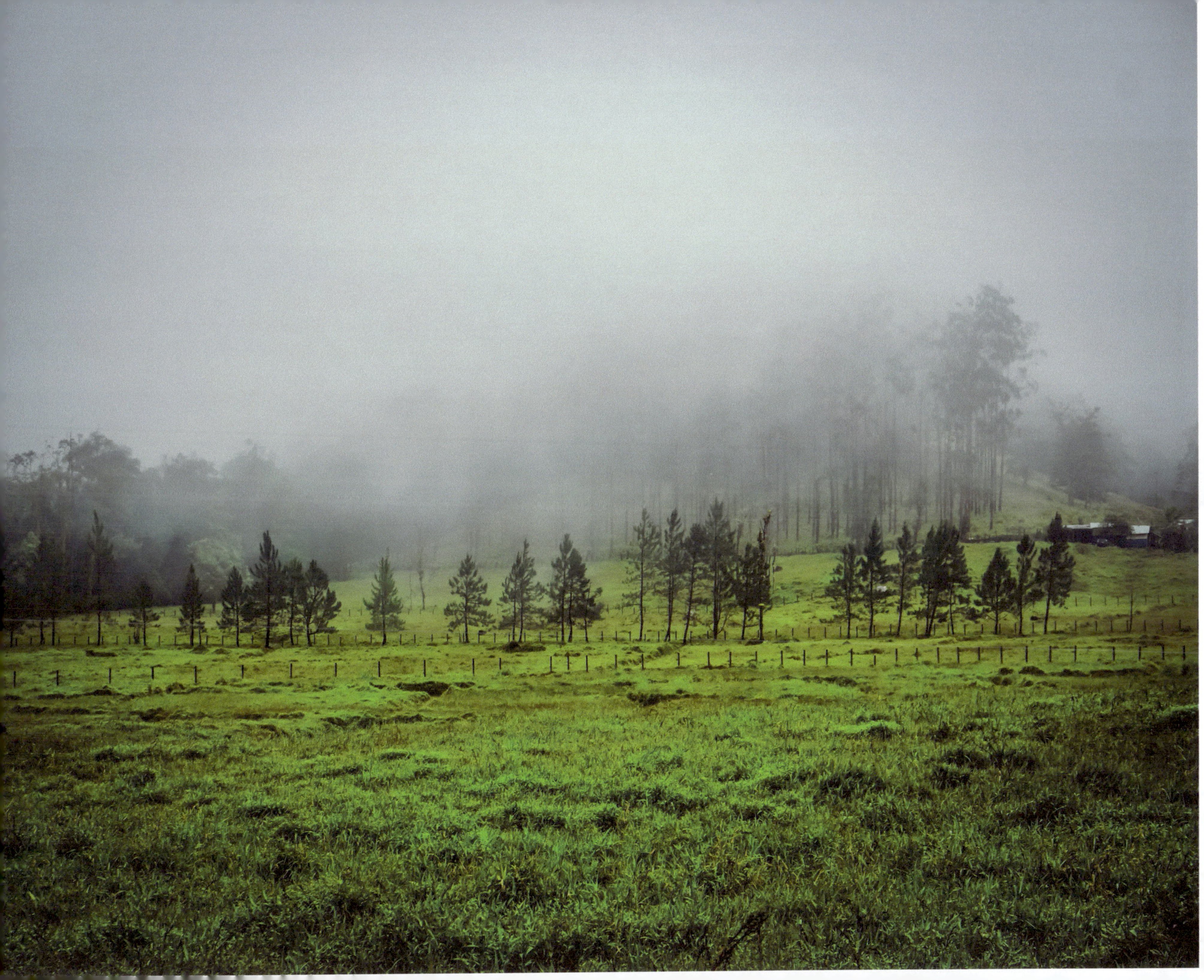

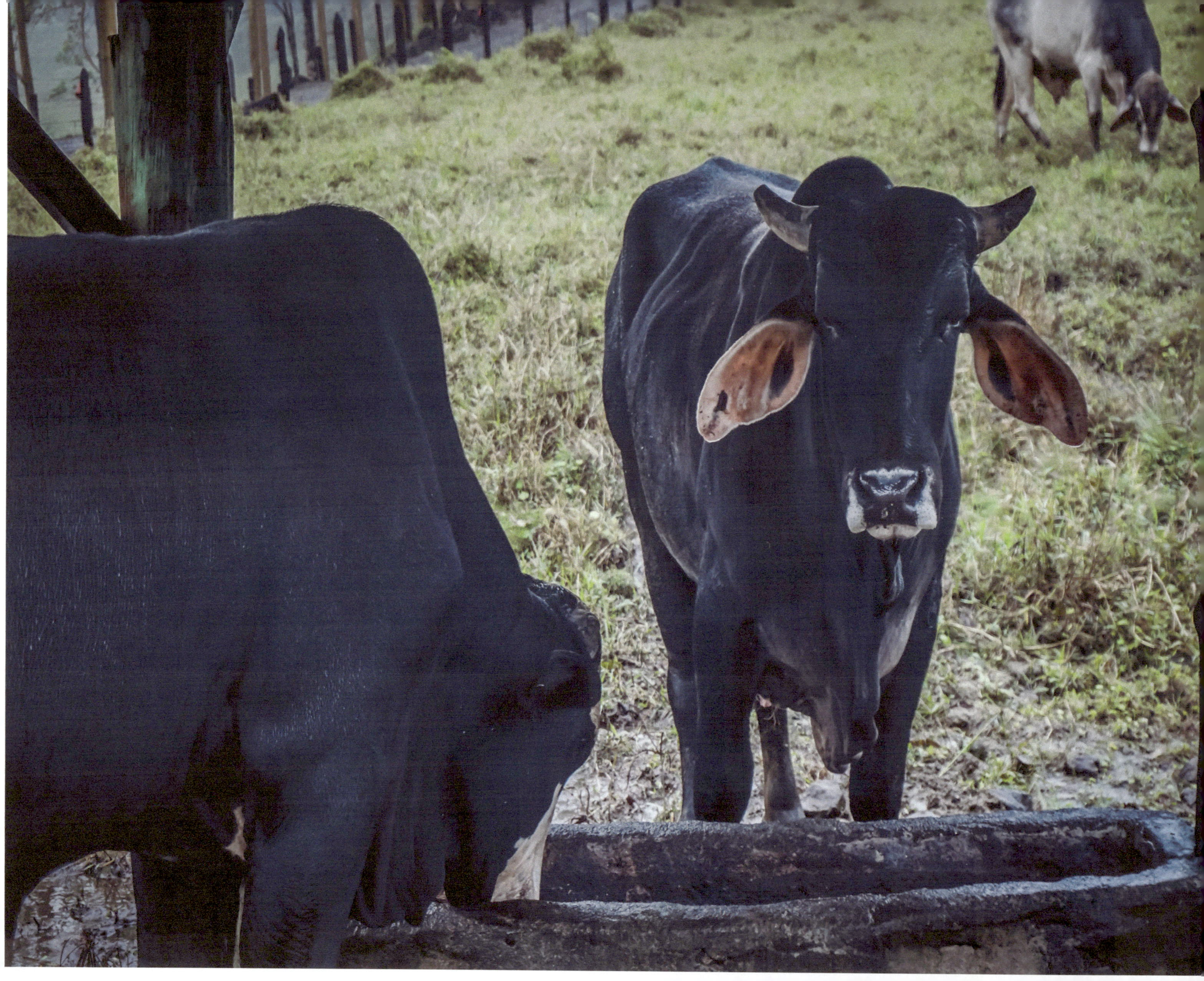

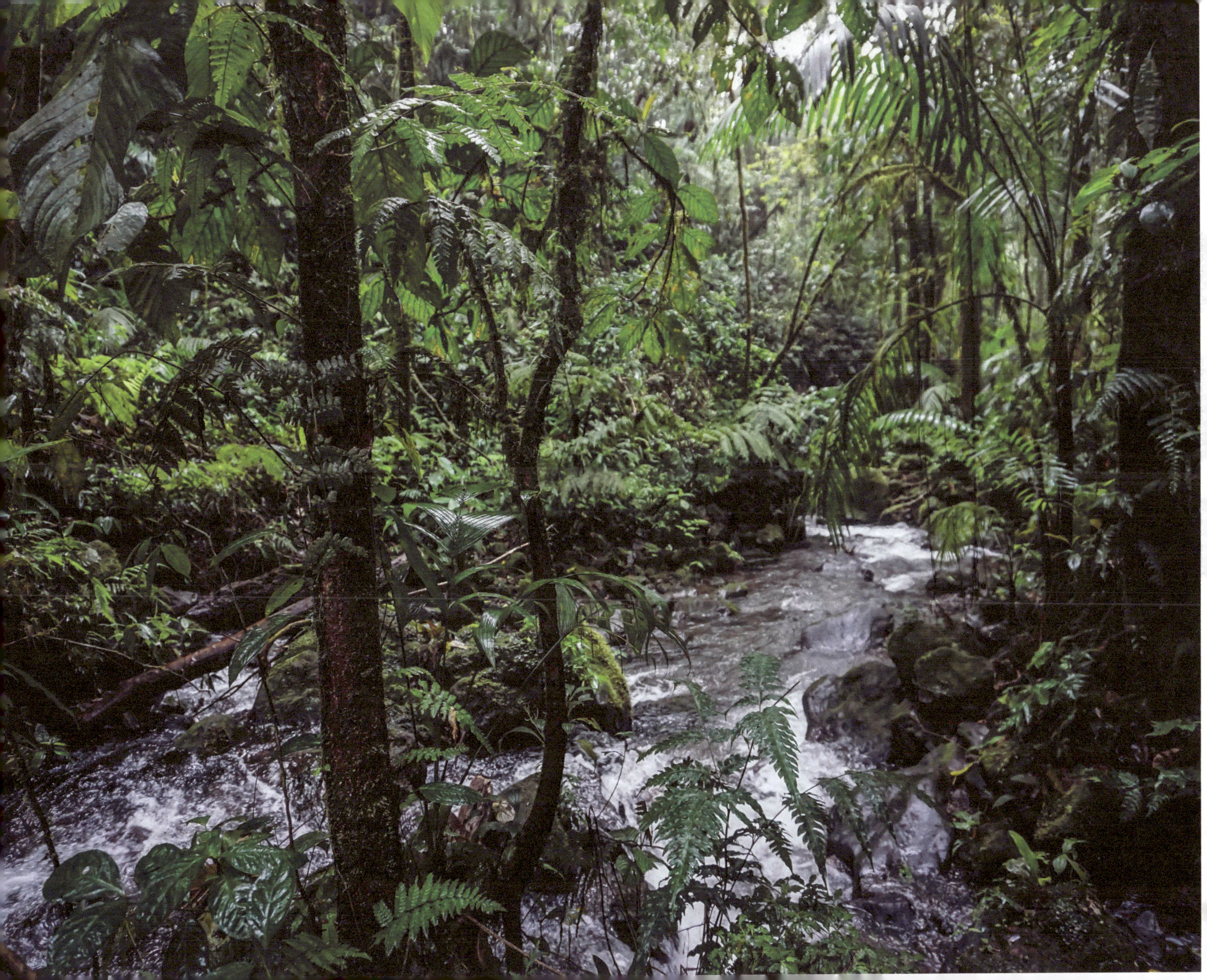

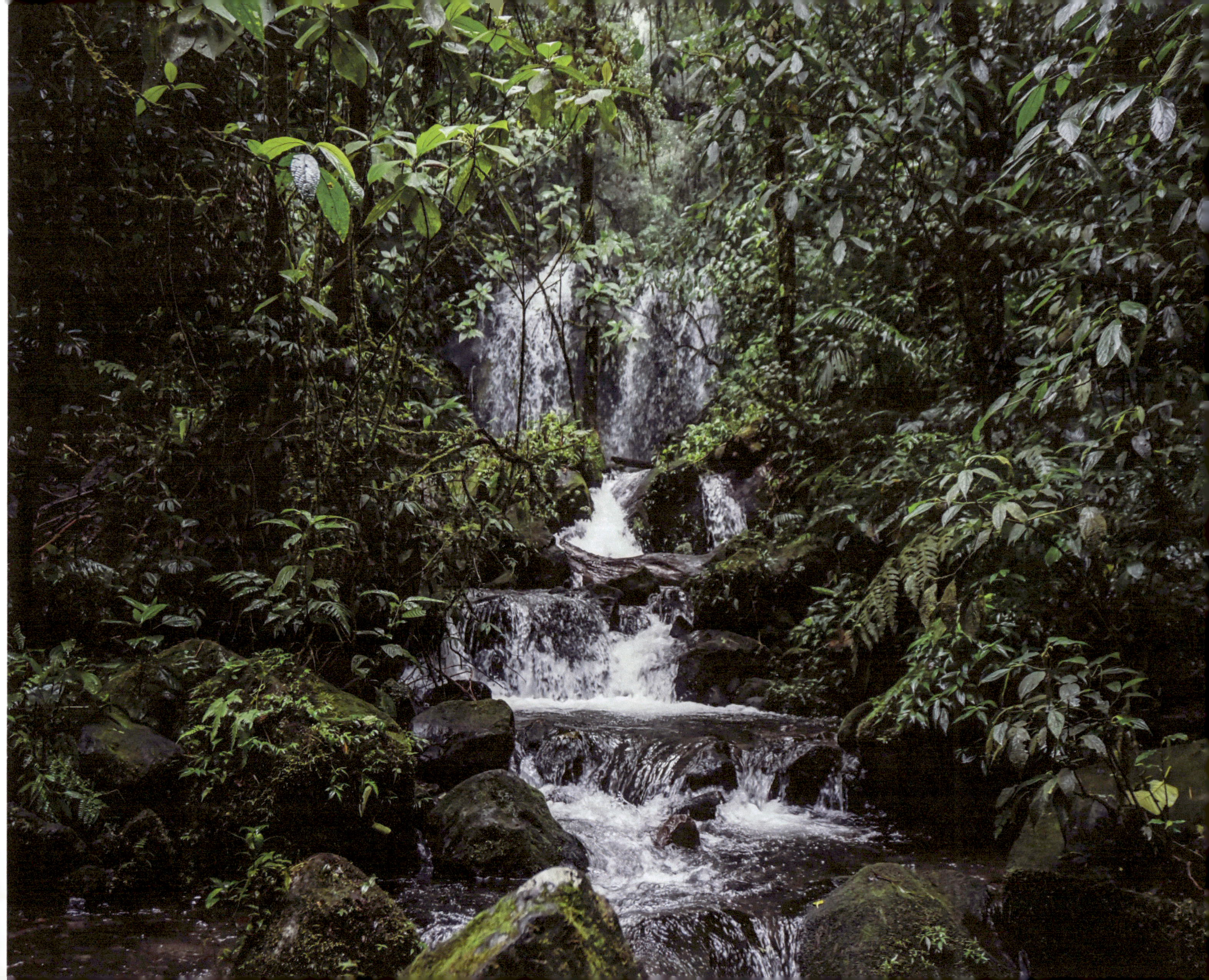

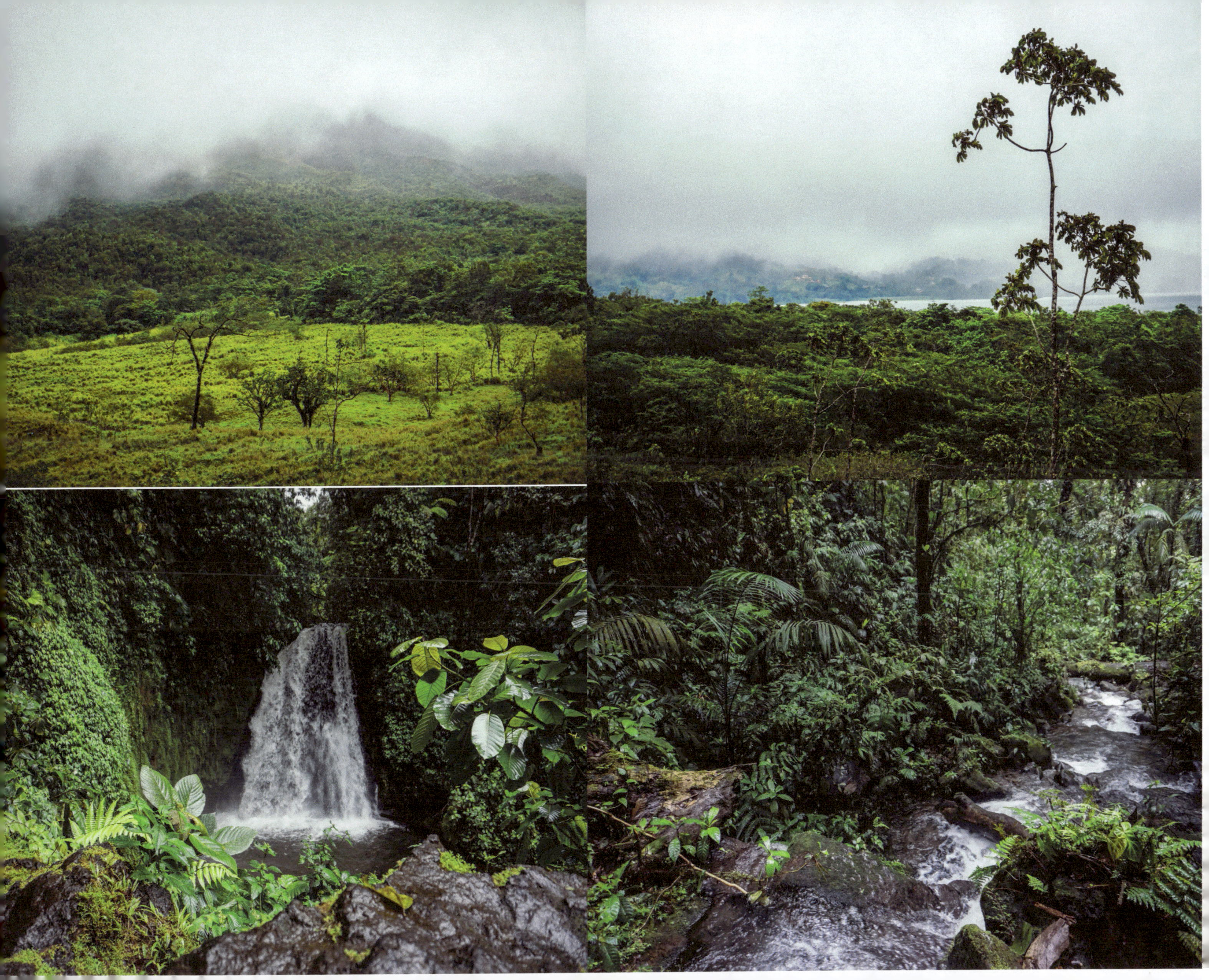

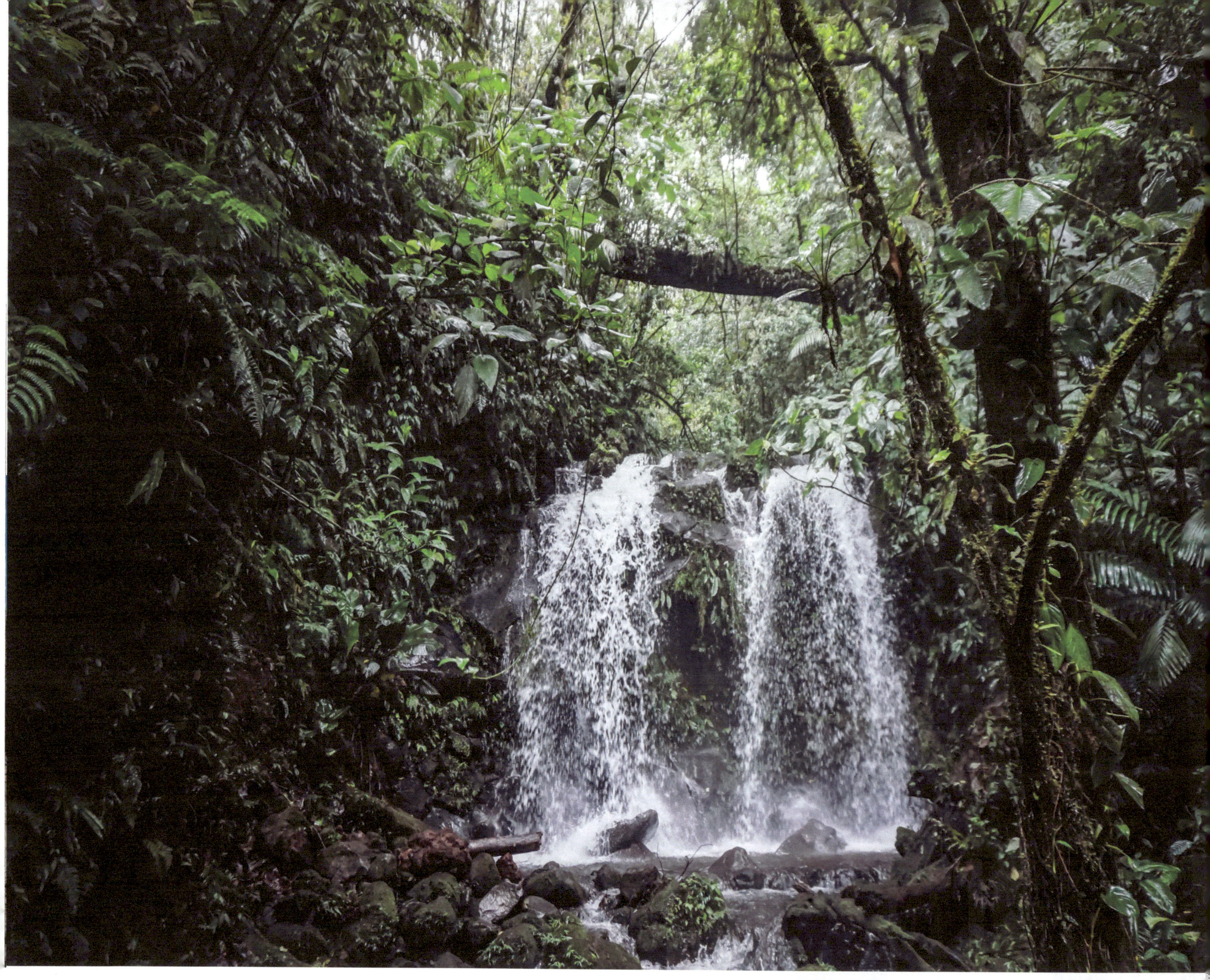

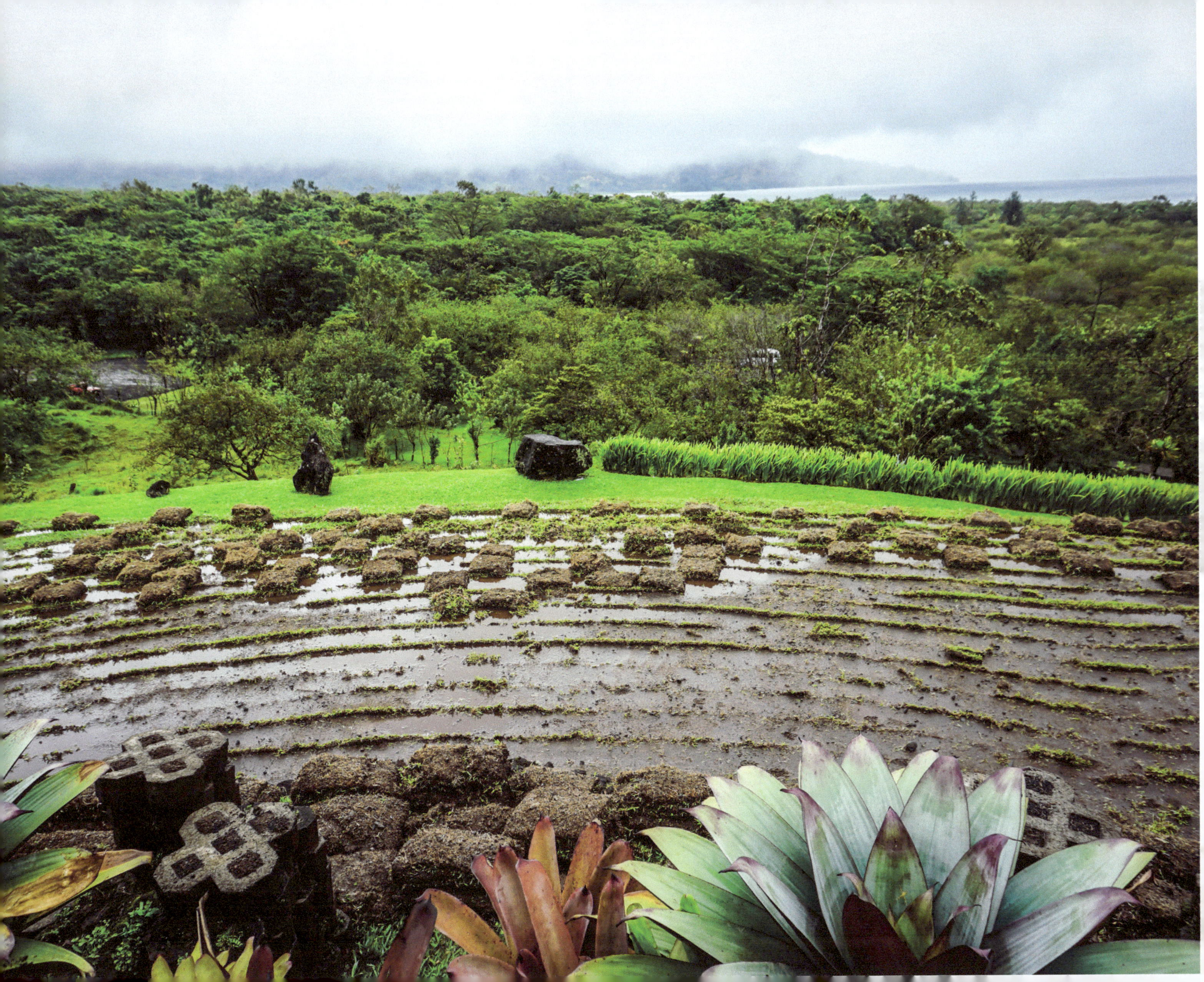

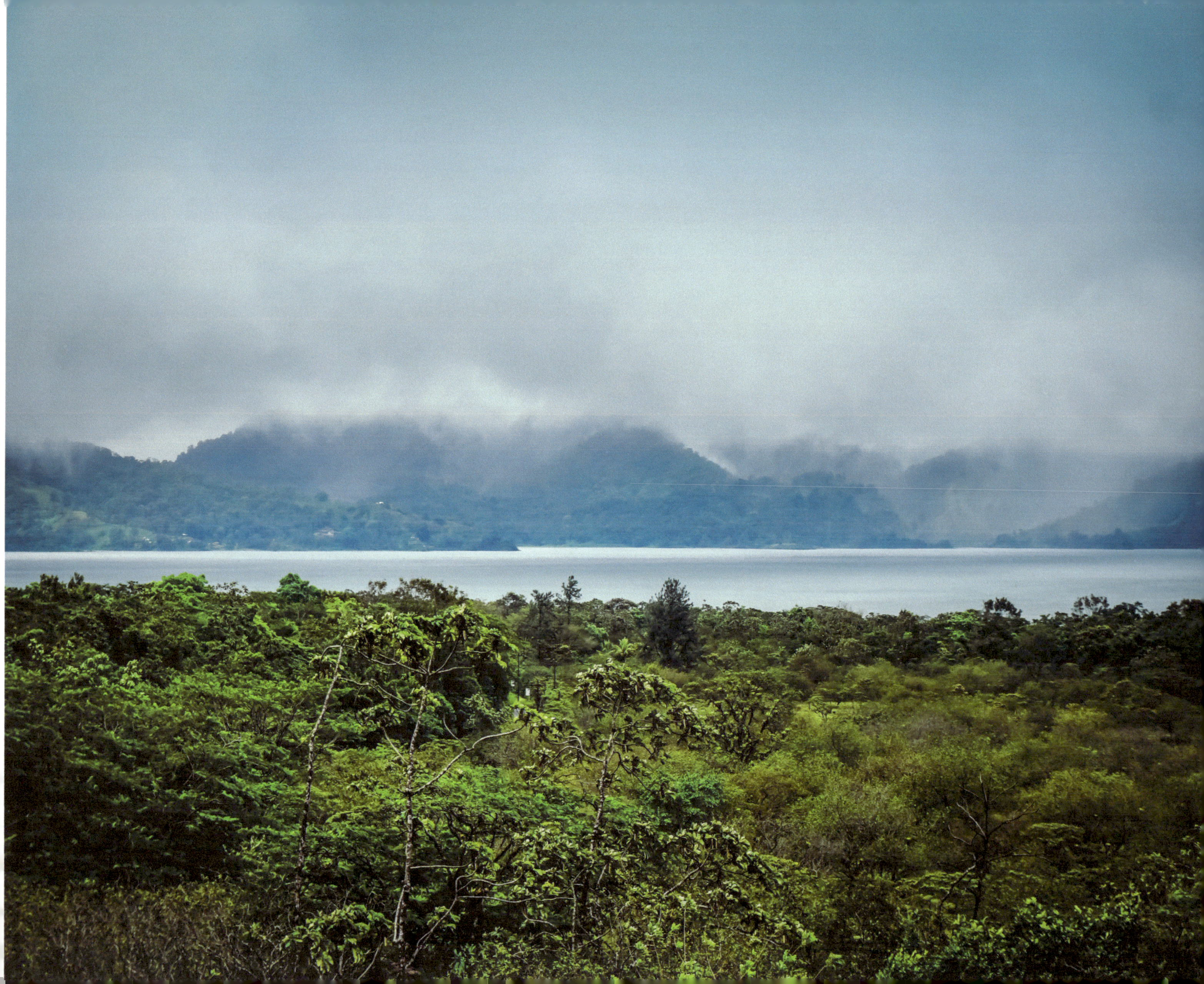

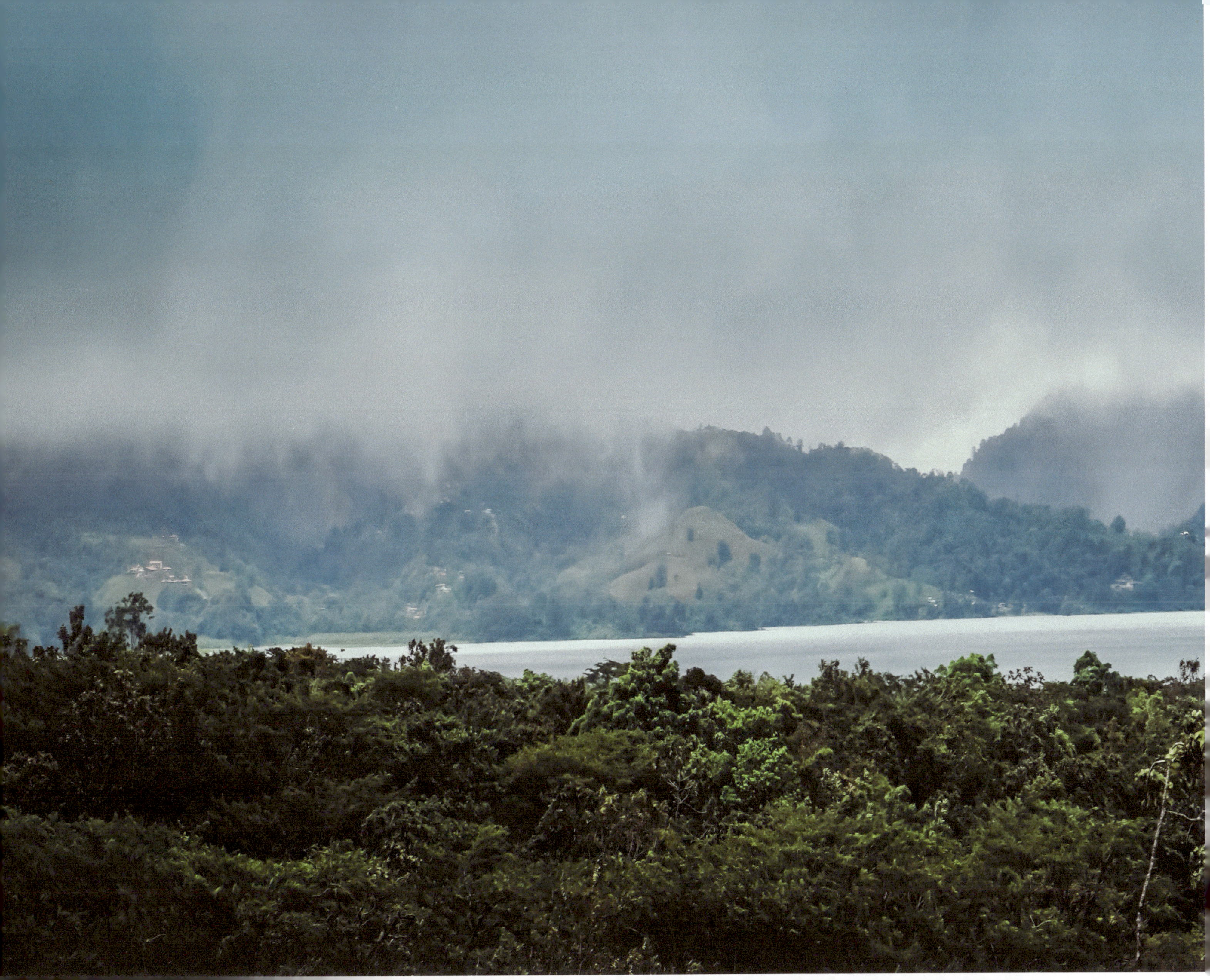

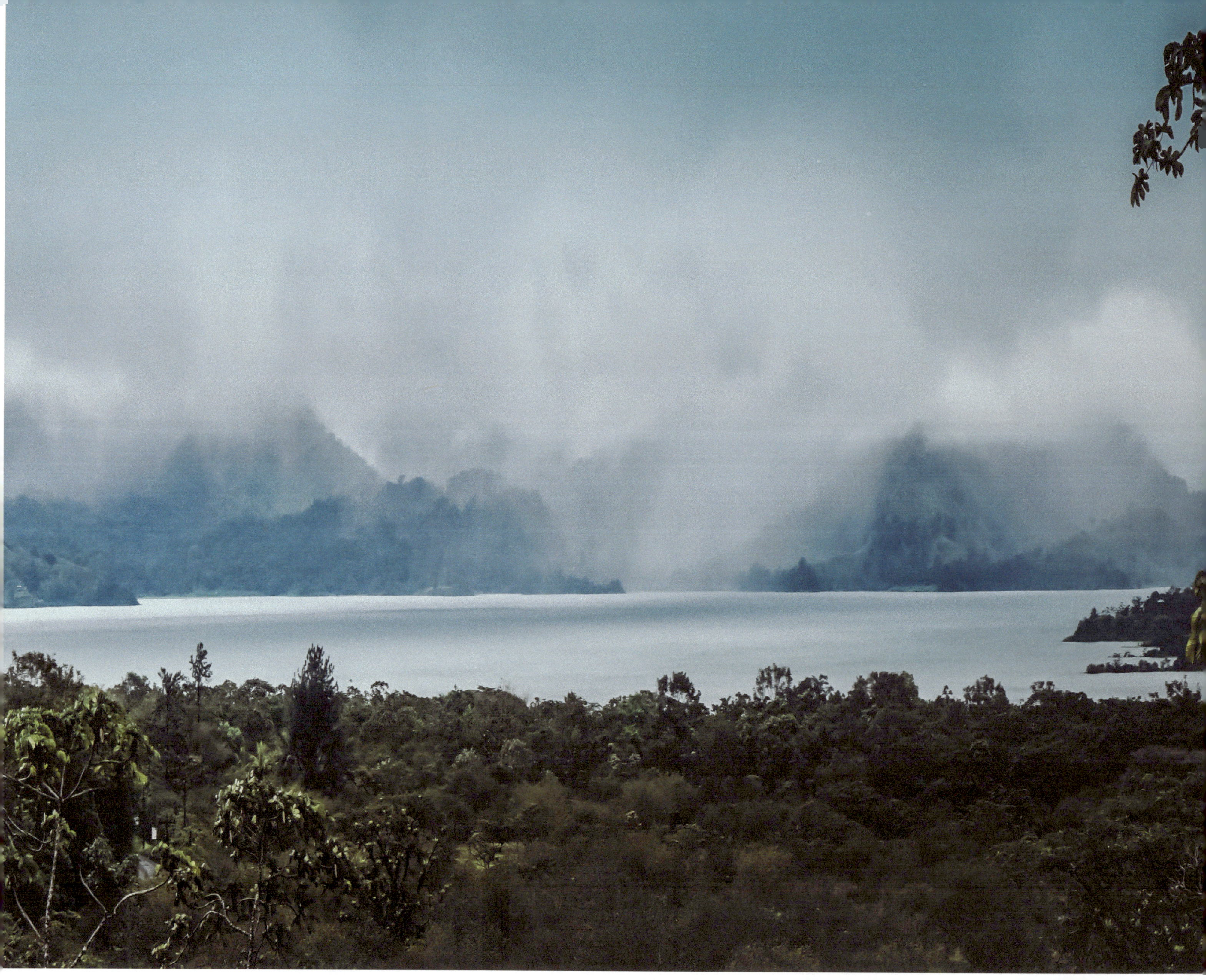

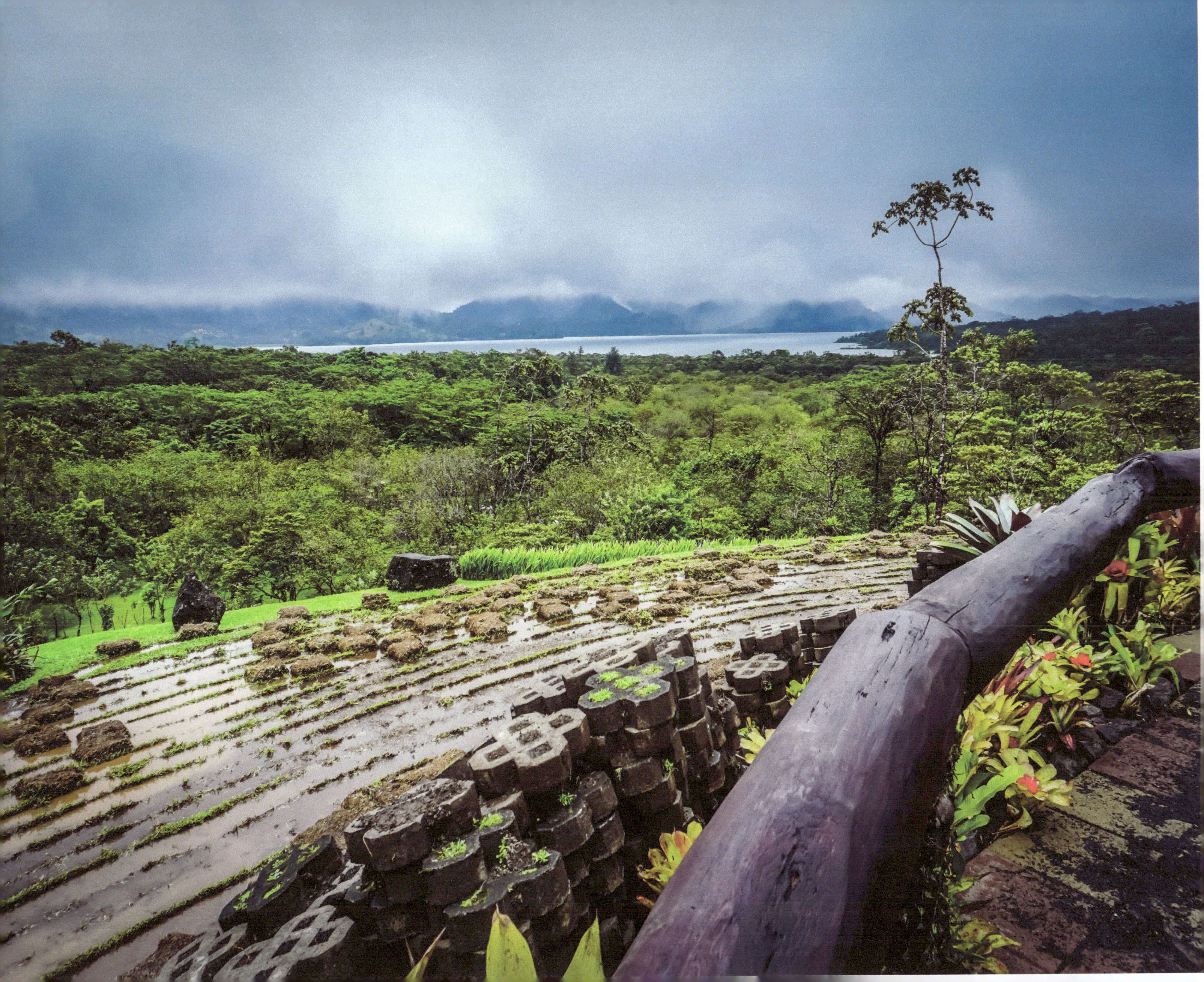

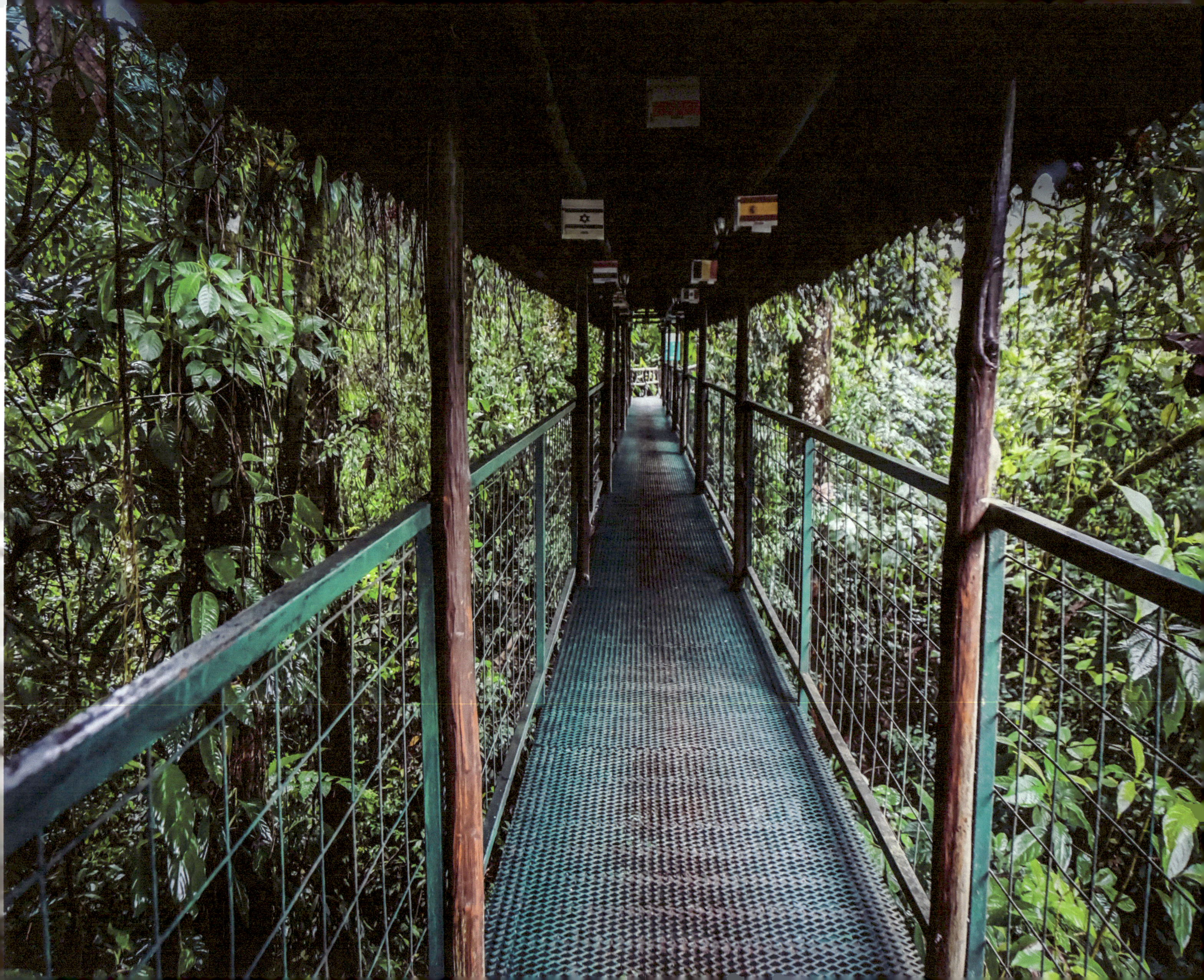

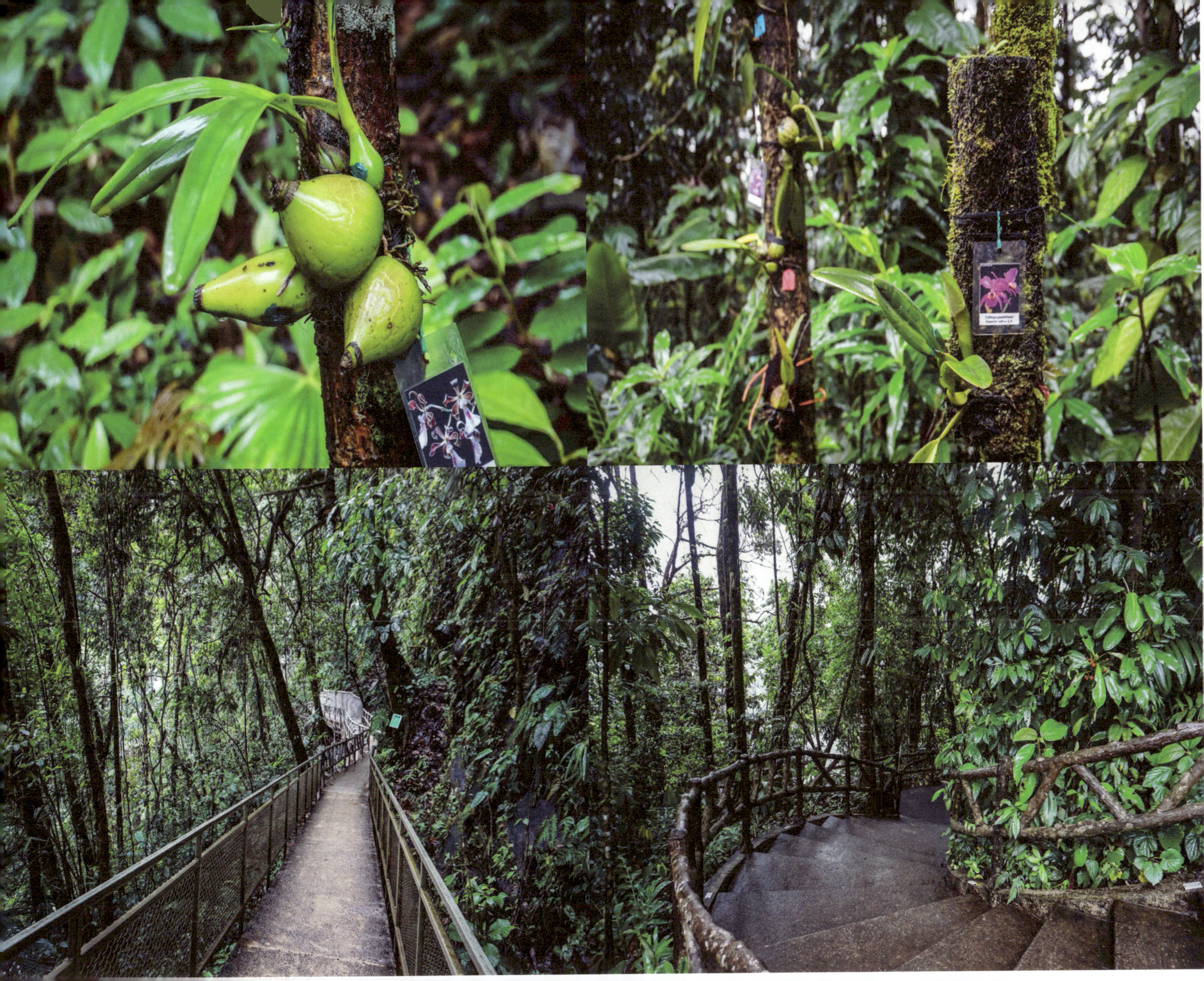

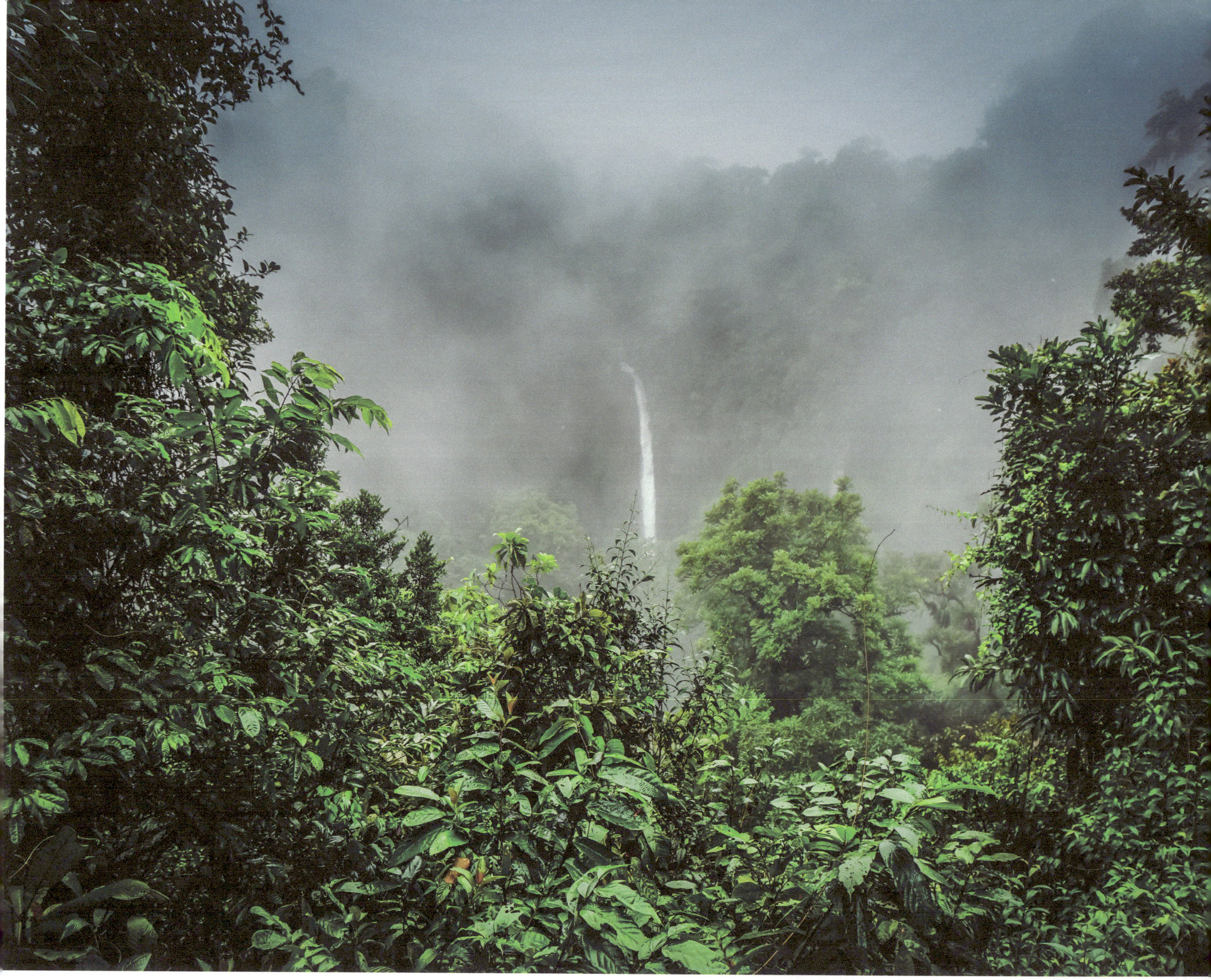

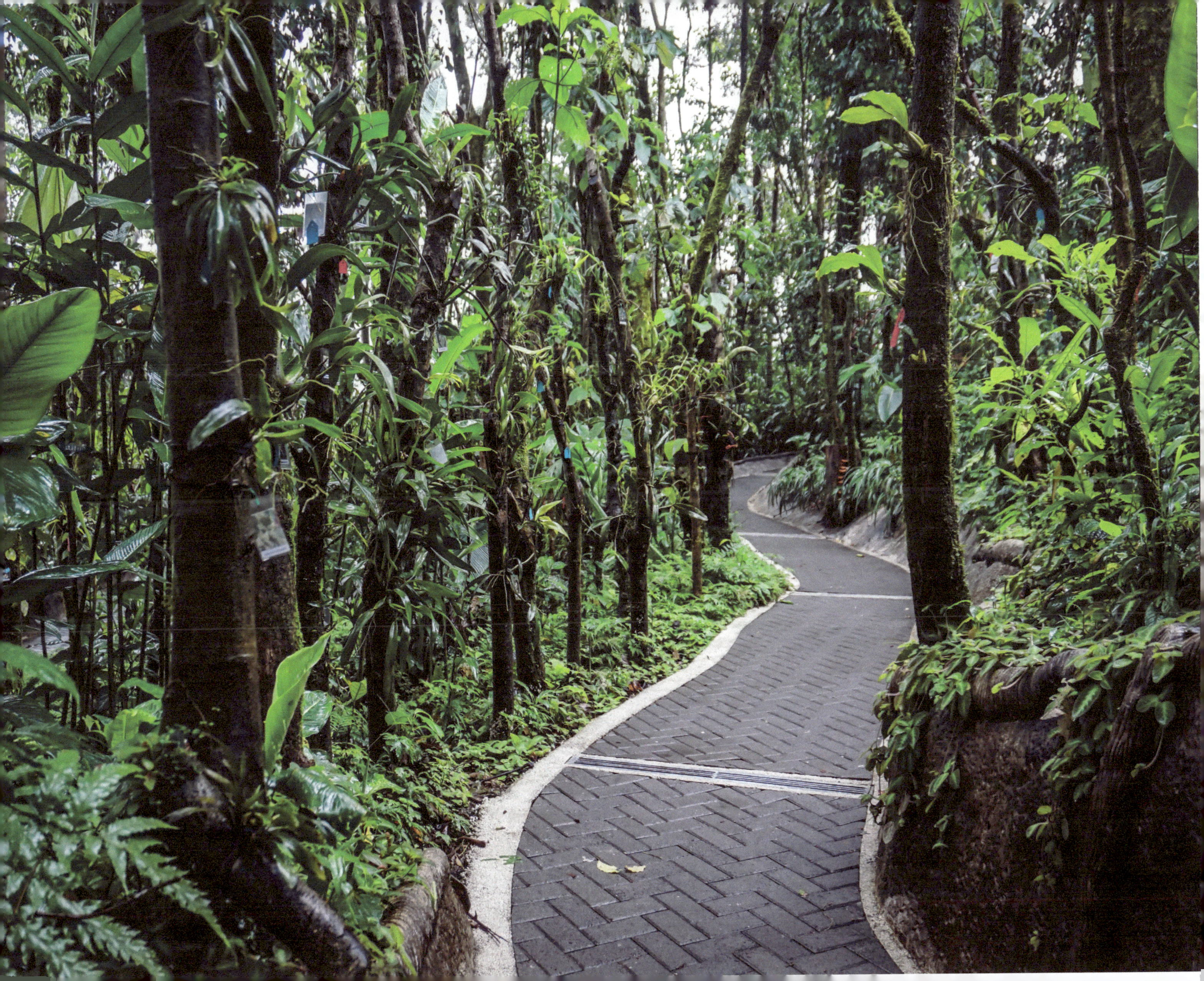

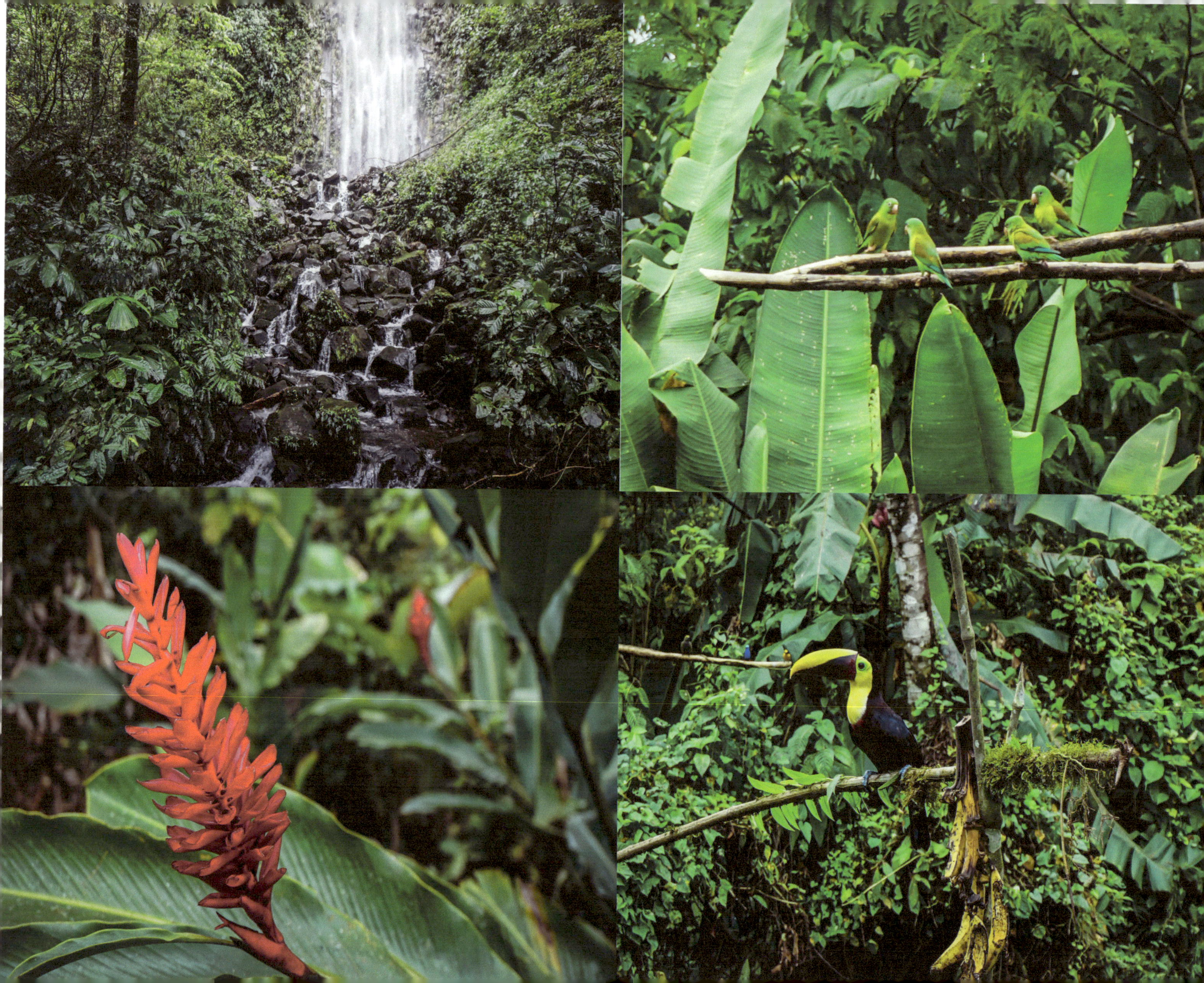

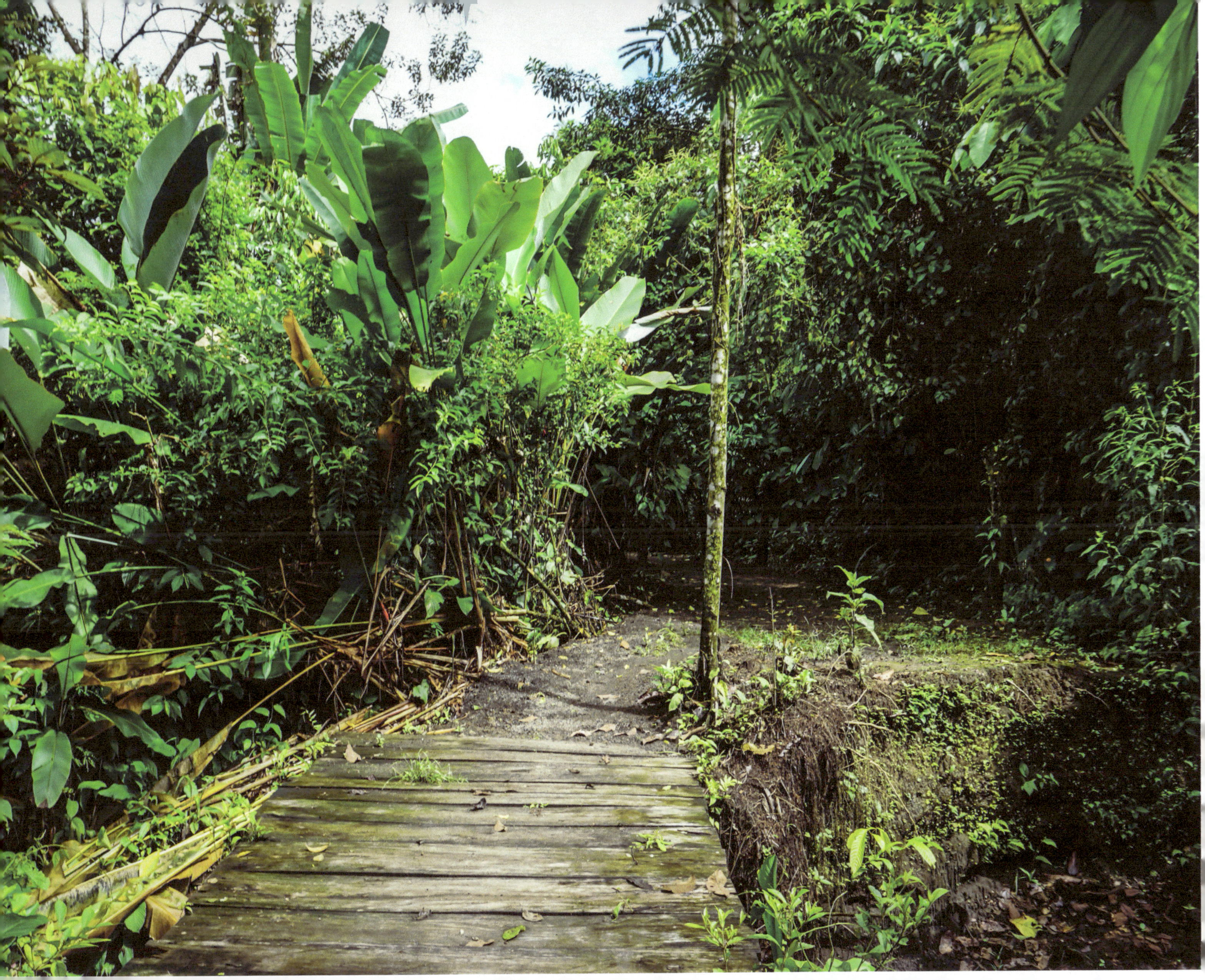

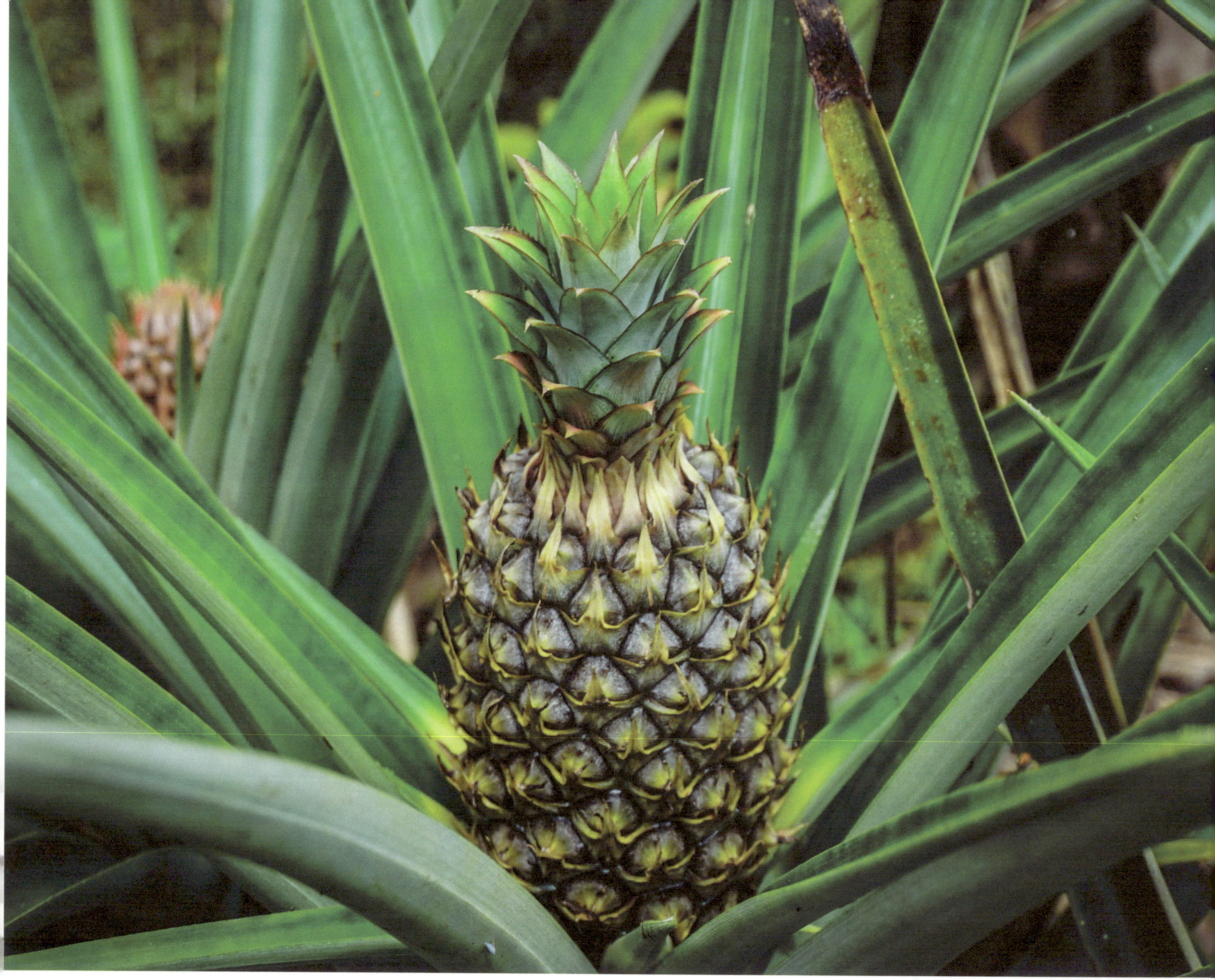

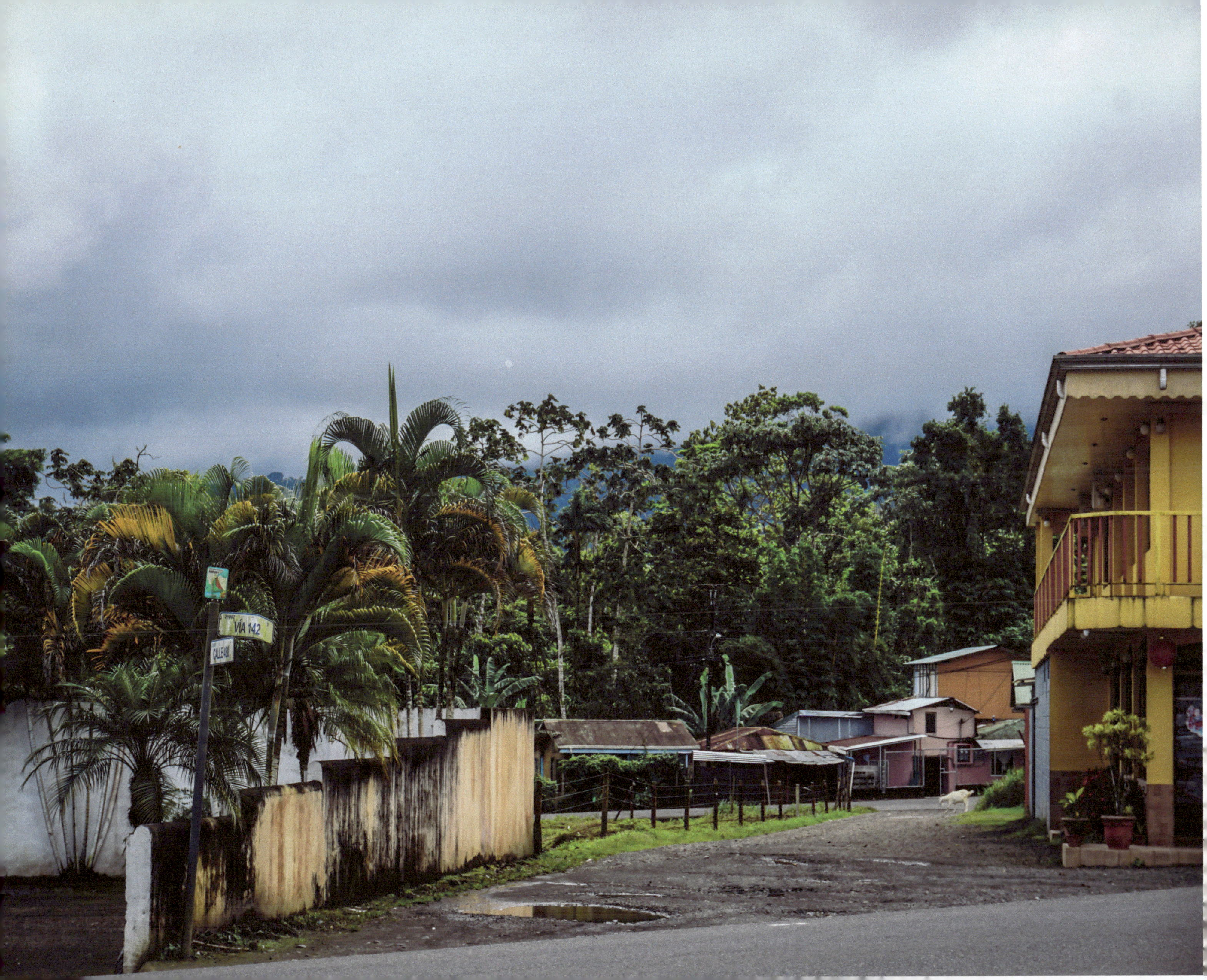

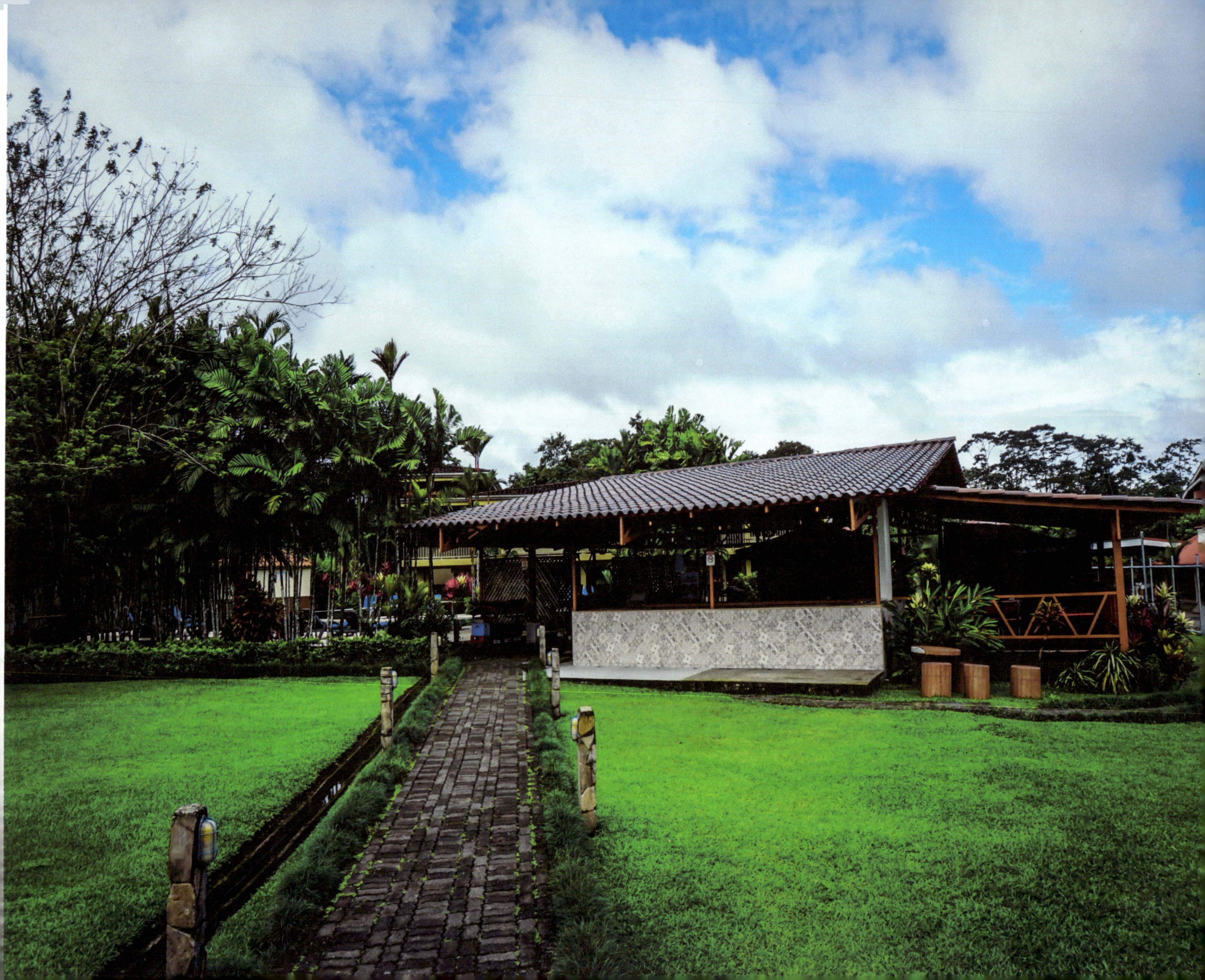

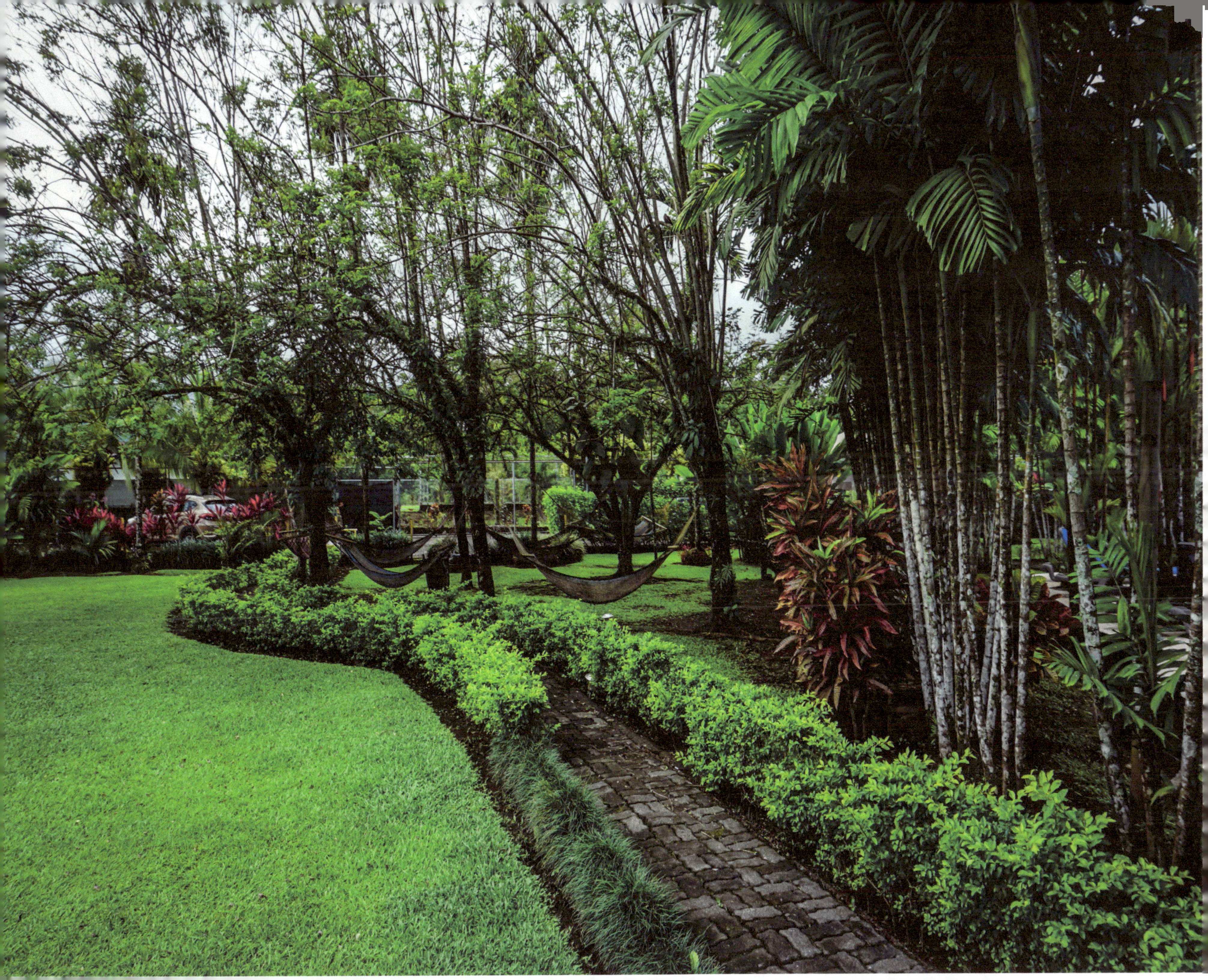

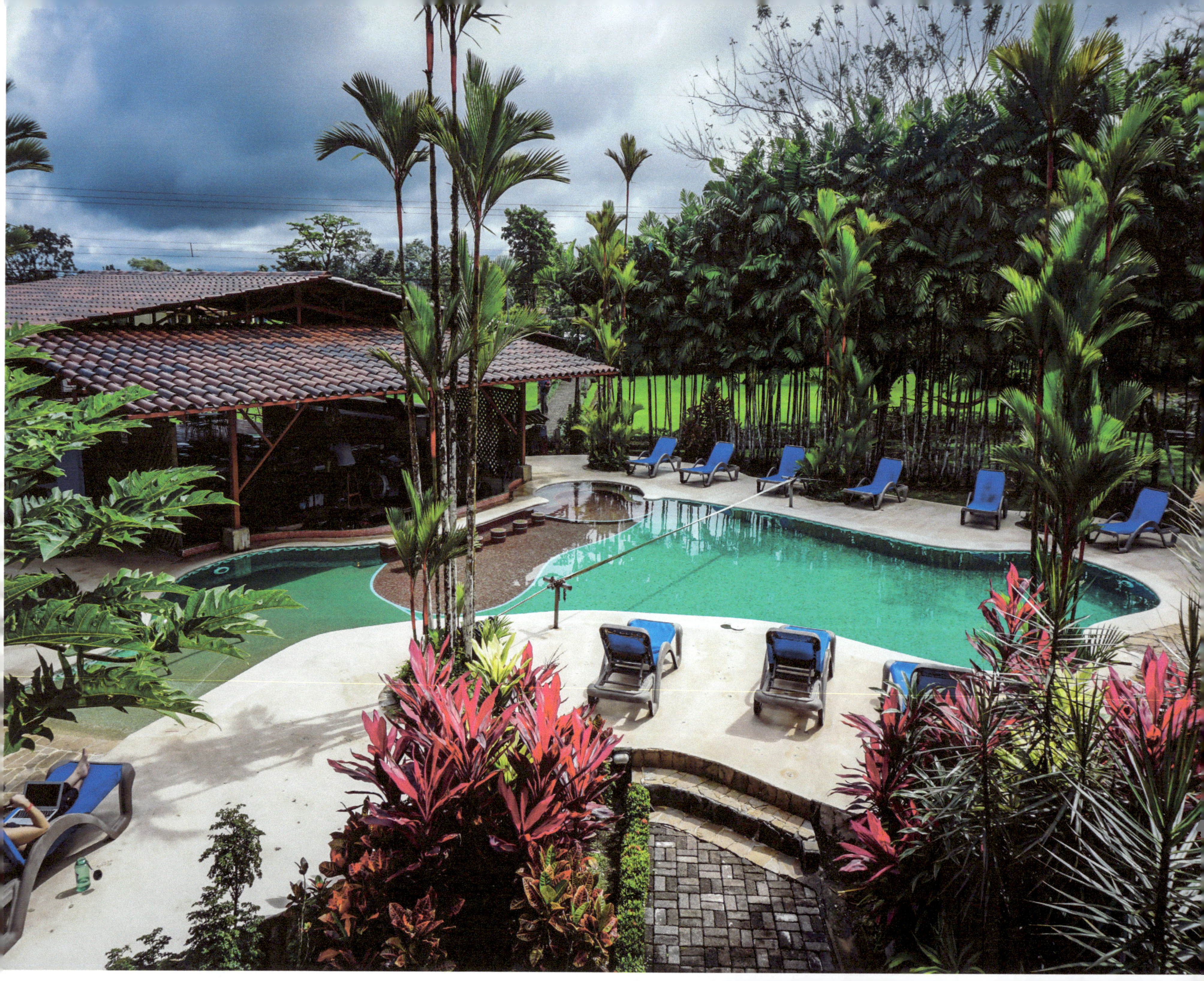

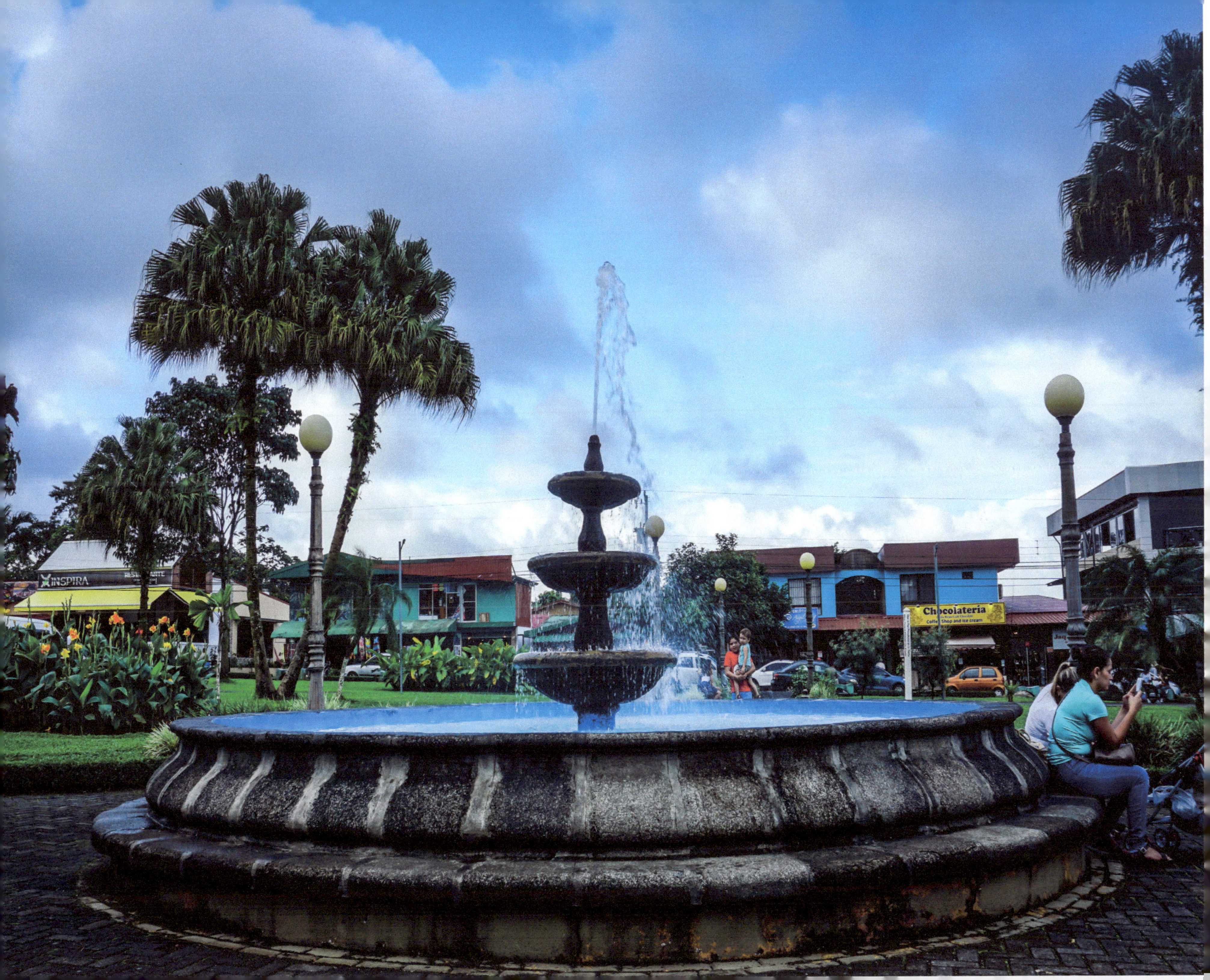
INSPIRA
Chocolateria
Coffee Shop and Ice cream

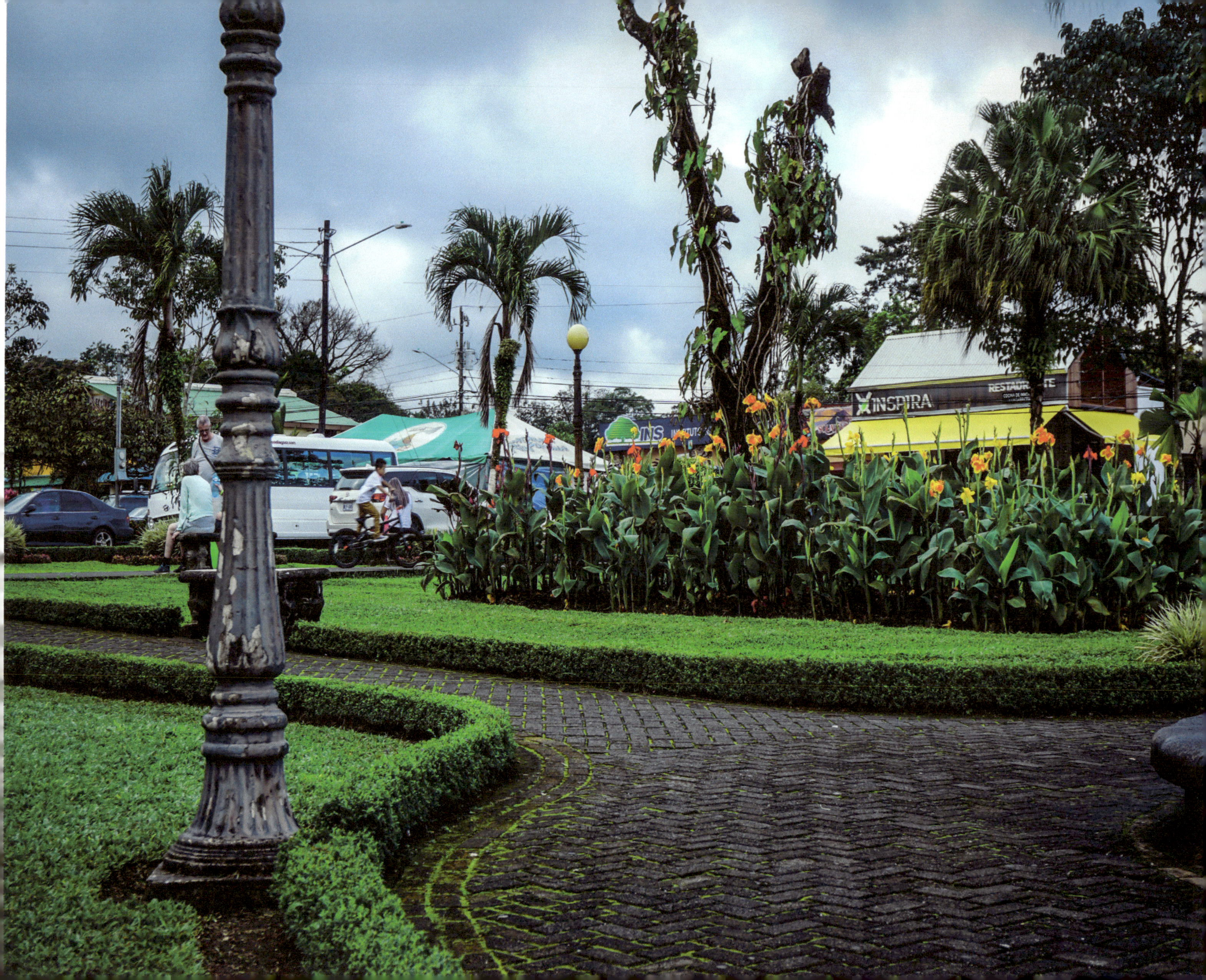
INSPIRA
RESTAURANTE
INS

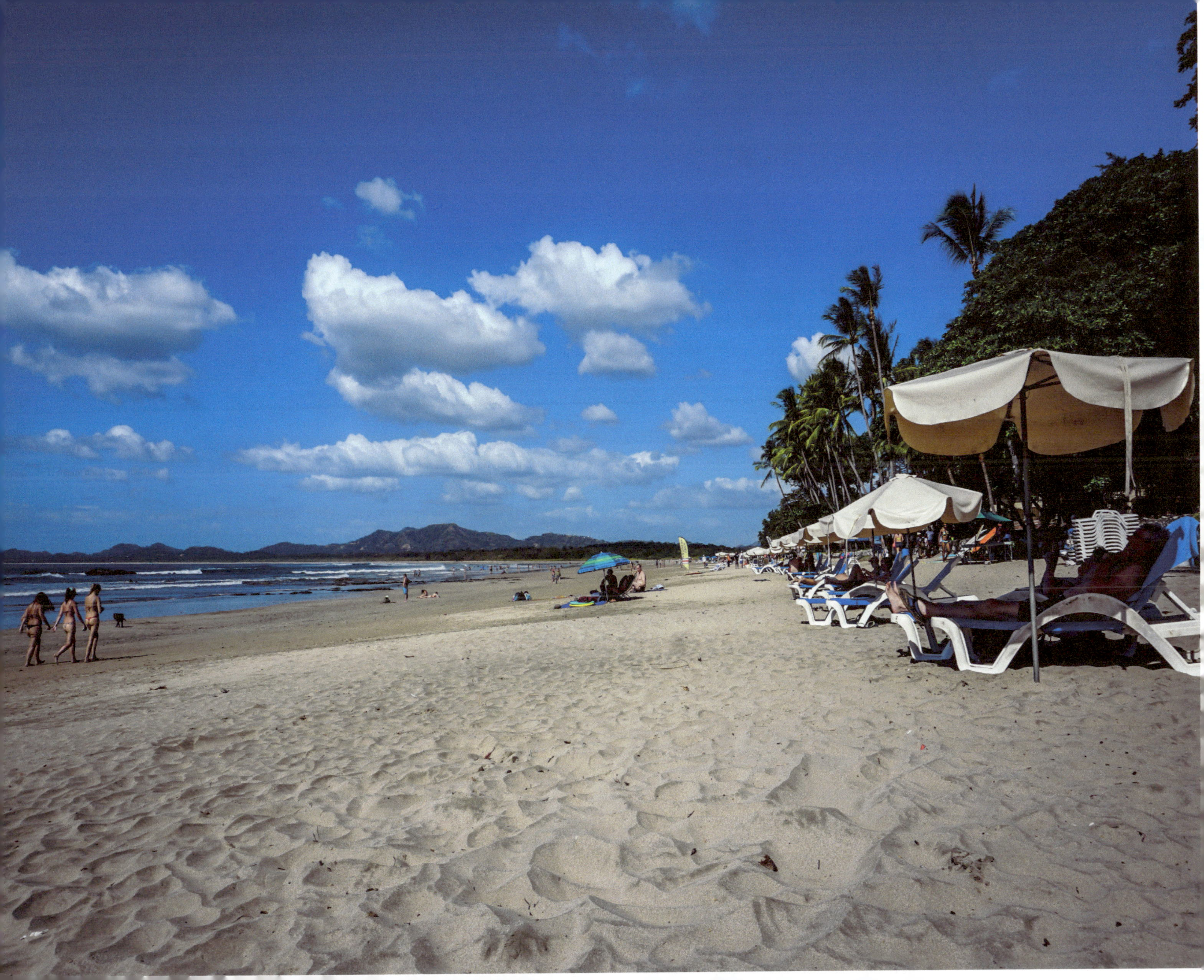

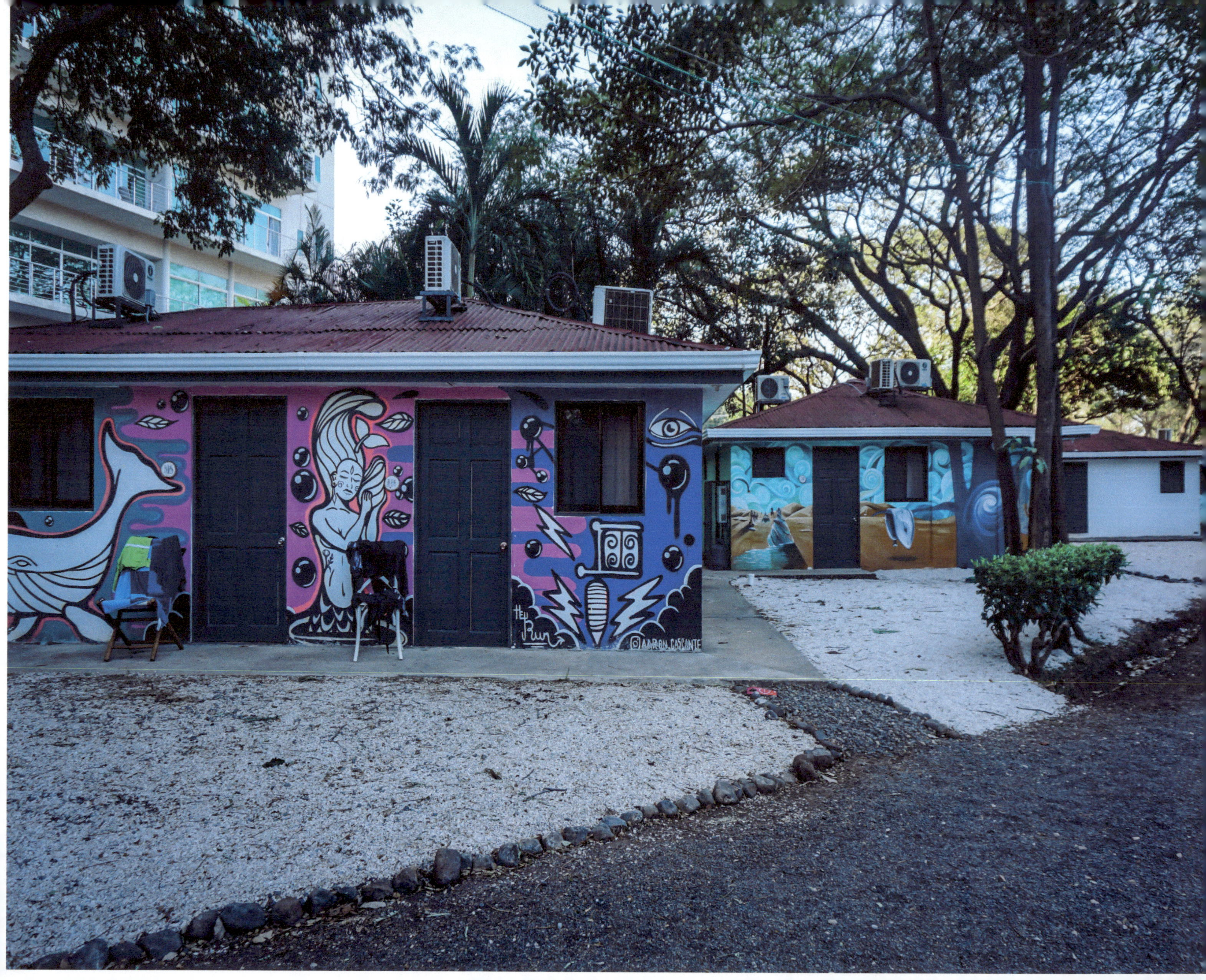

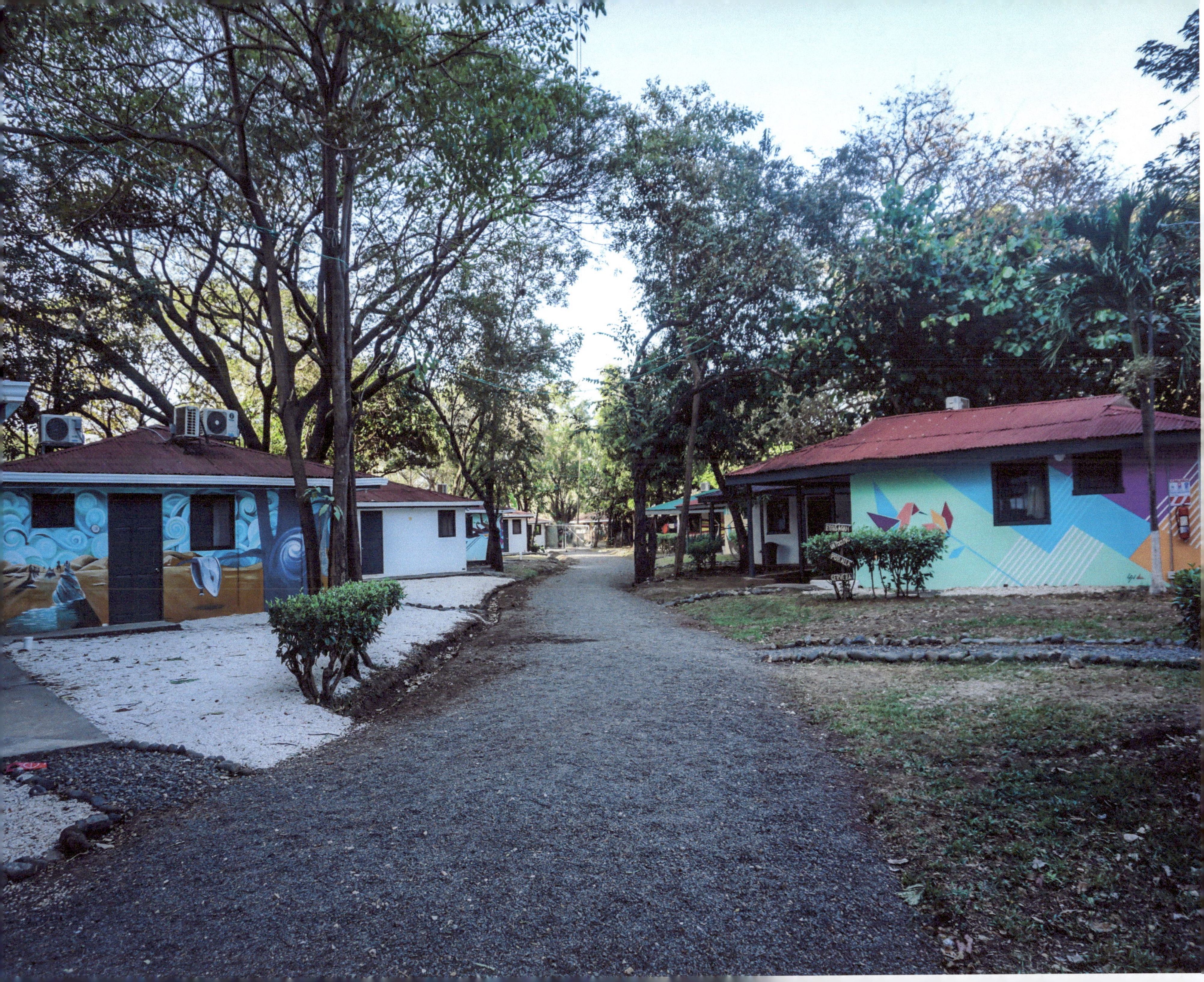

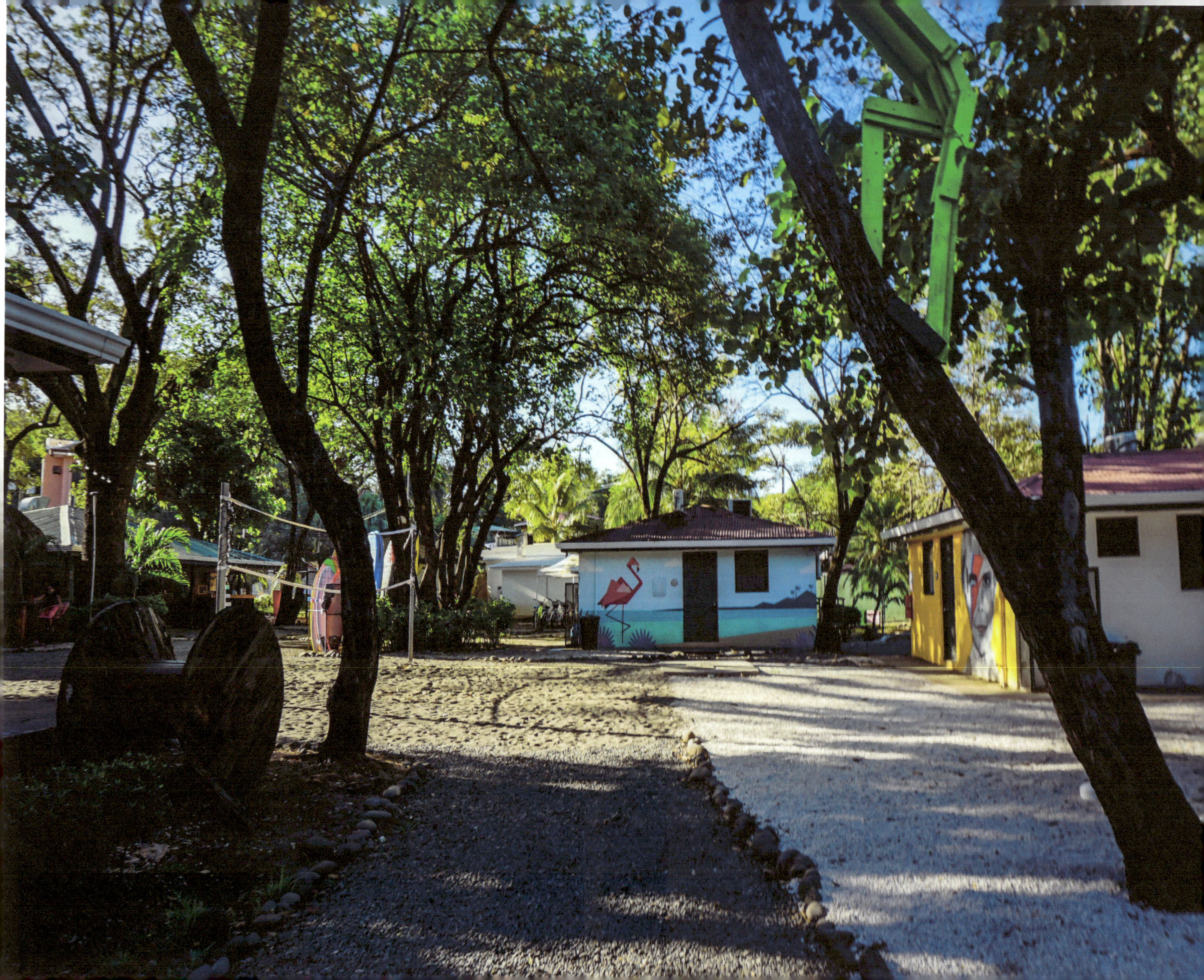

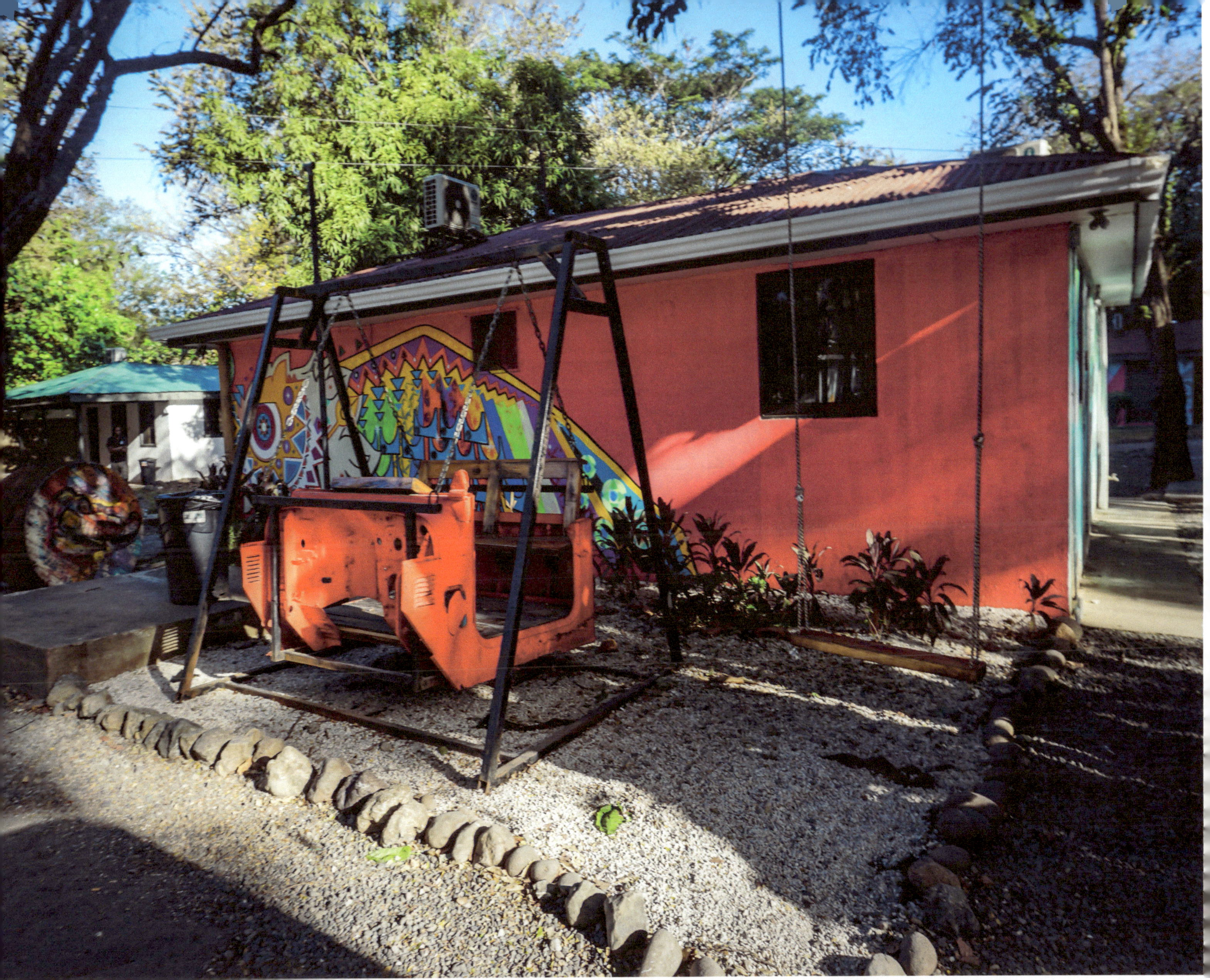

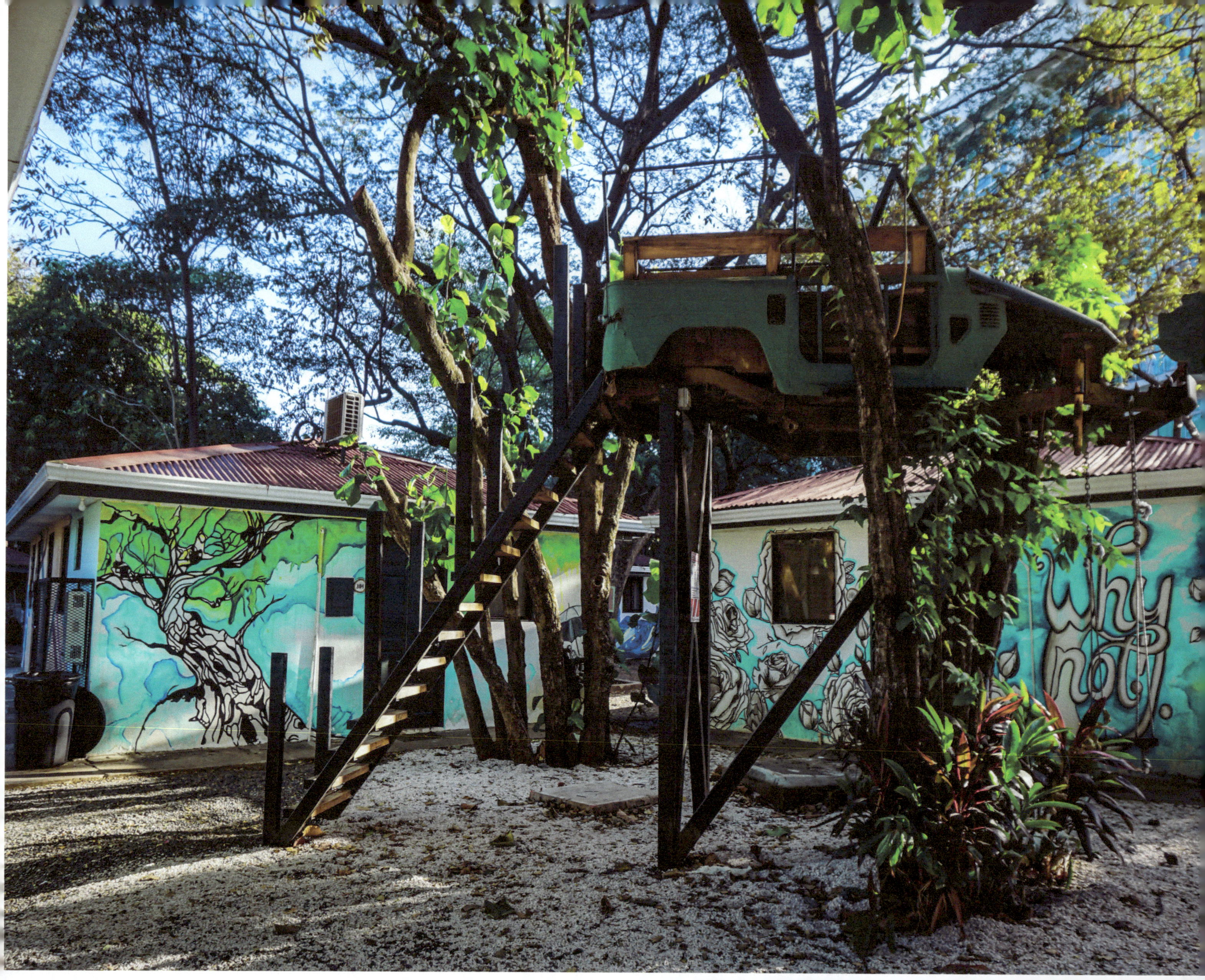

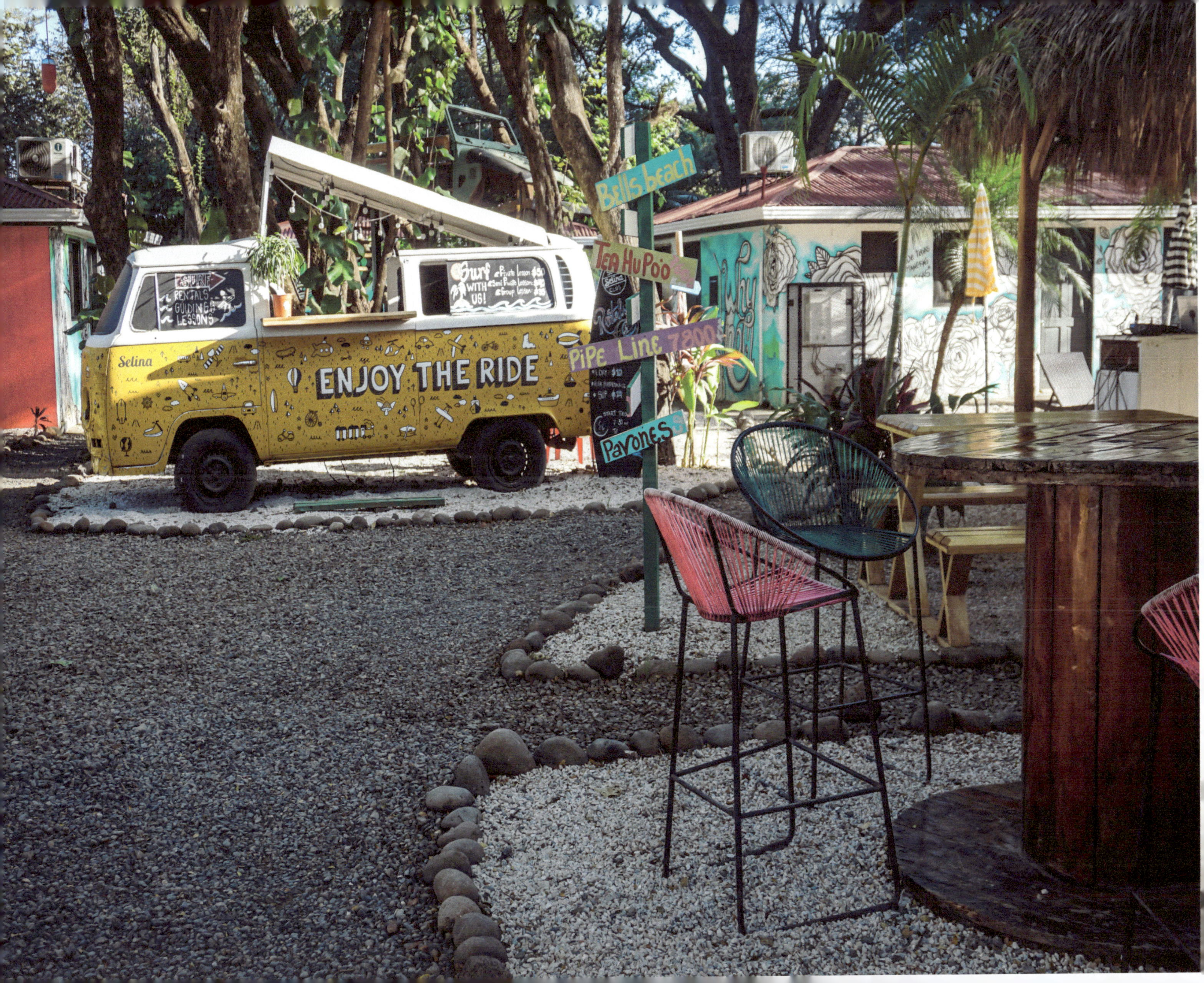

Bells Beach
Tea Hu Poo
Pipe Line 7800
Payones
Surf
RENTALS
GUIDING &
LESSONS
Surf WITH US!
Private Lesson $50
Semi Privte Lesson $40
Group Lesson $35
Selina
ENJOY THE RIDE

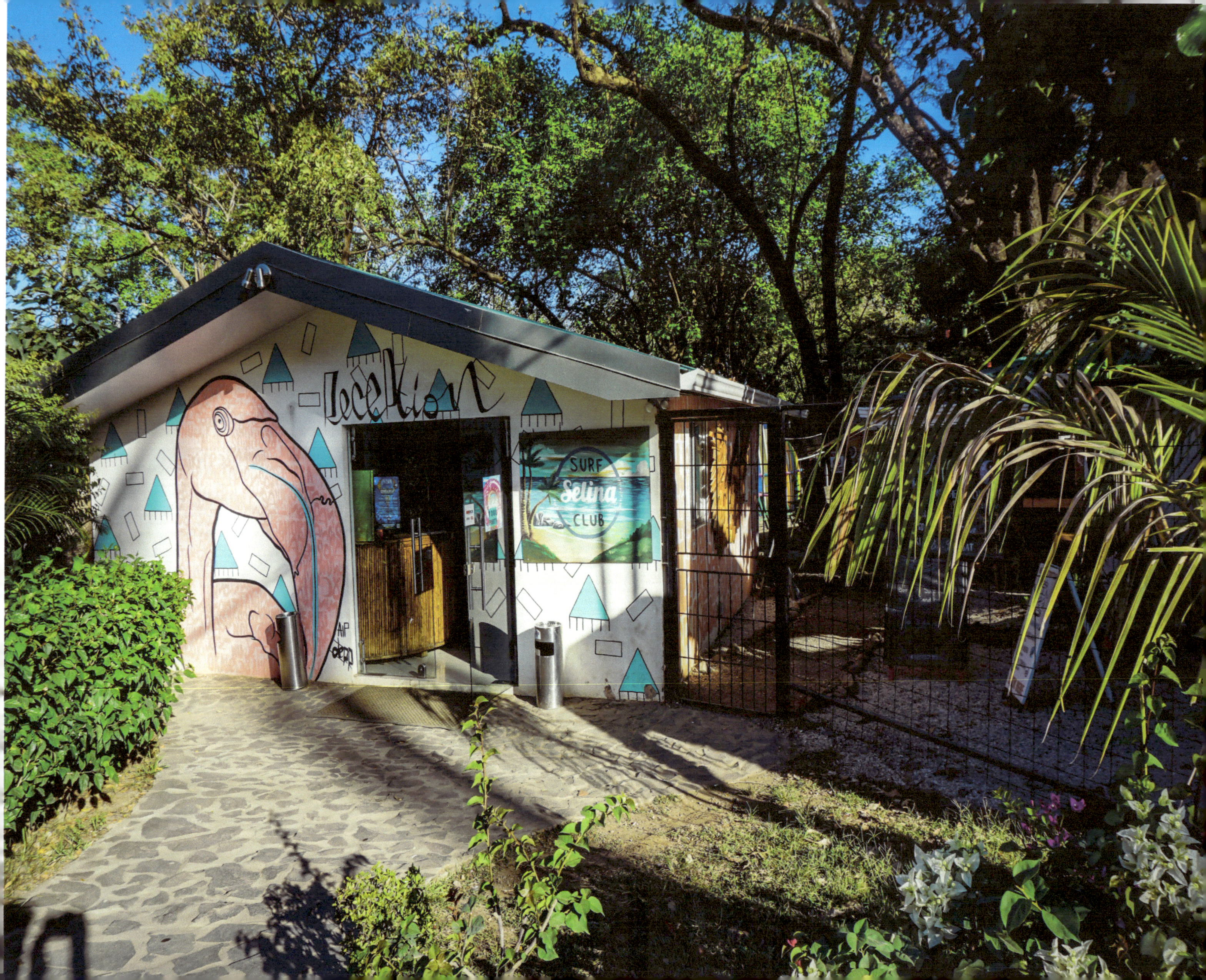
reception
SURF
Selina
CLUB

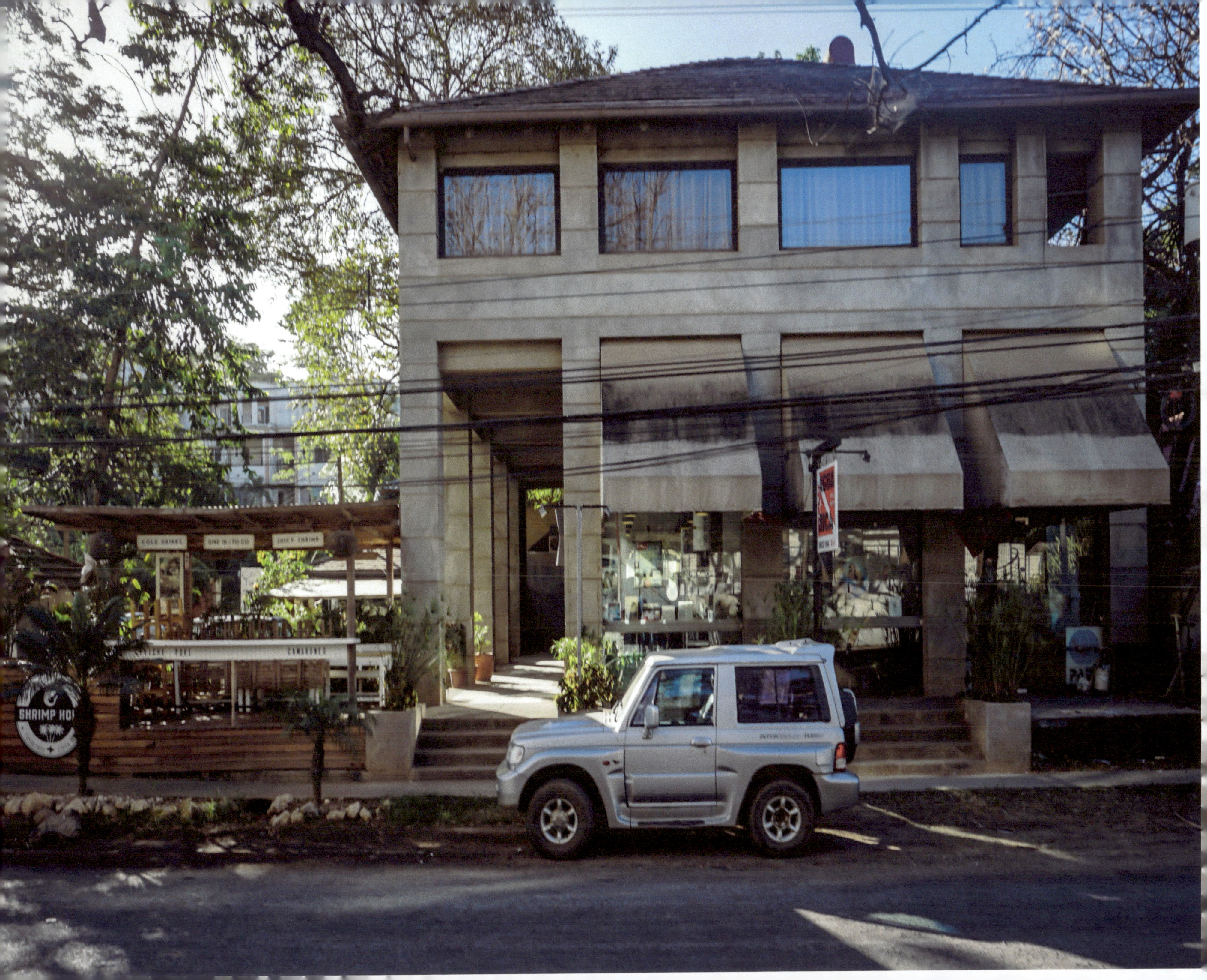

COLD DRINKS
DINE IN · TO GO
JUICY SHRIMP
CEVICHE POKE
CAMARONES
SHRIMP HO

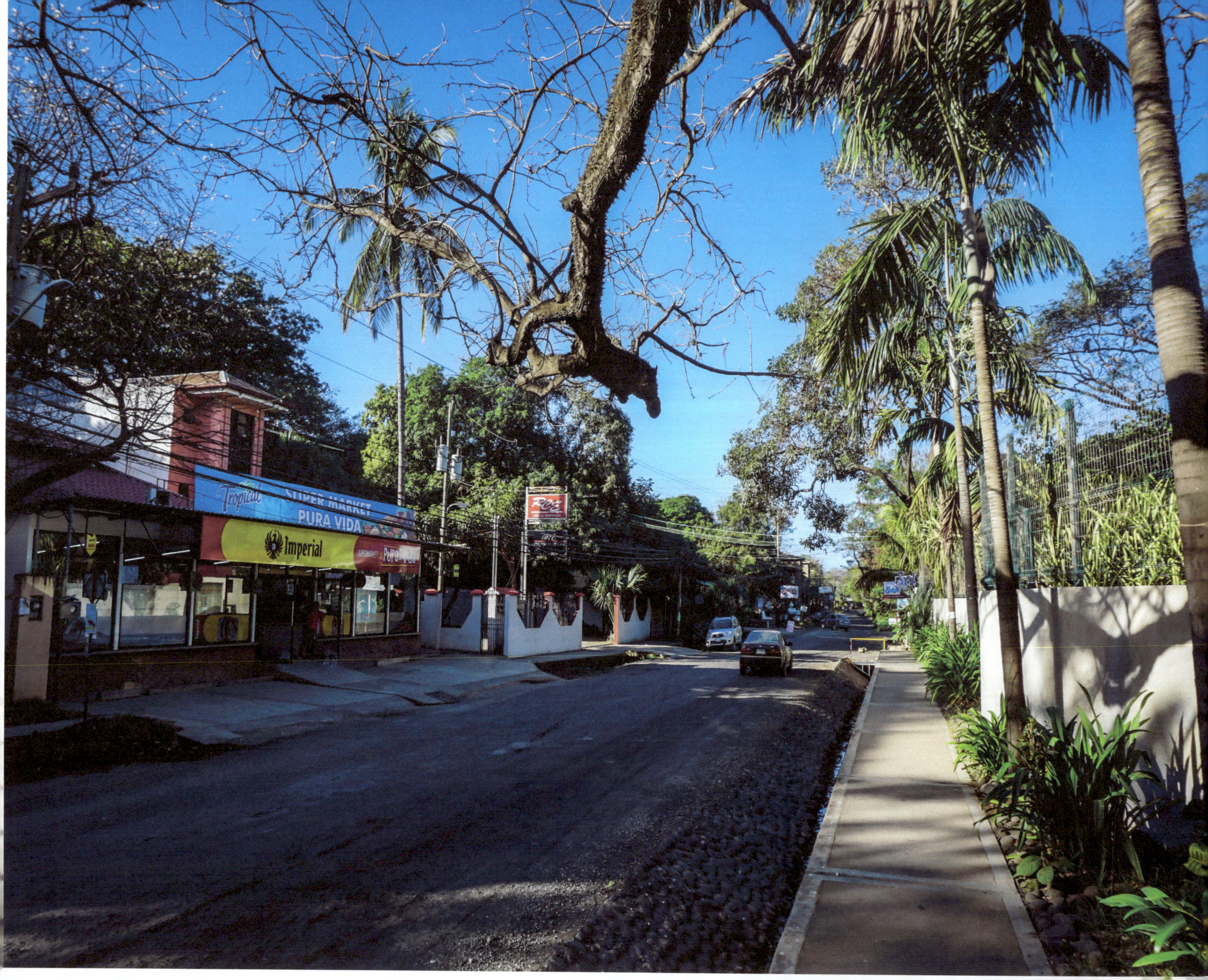
Tropical
SUPER MARKET
PURA VIDA
Imperial
Pura Vida

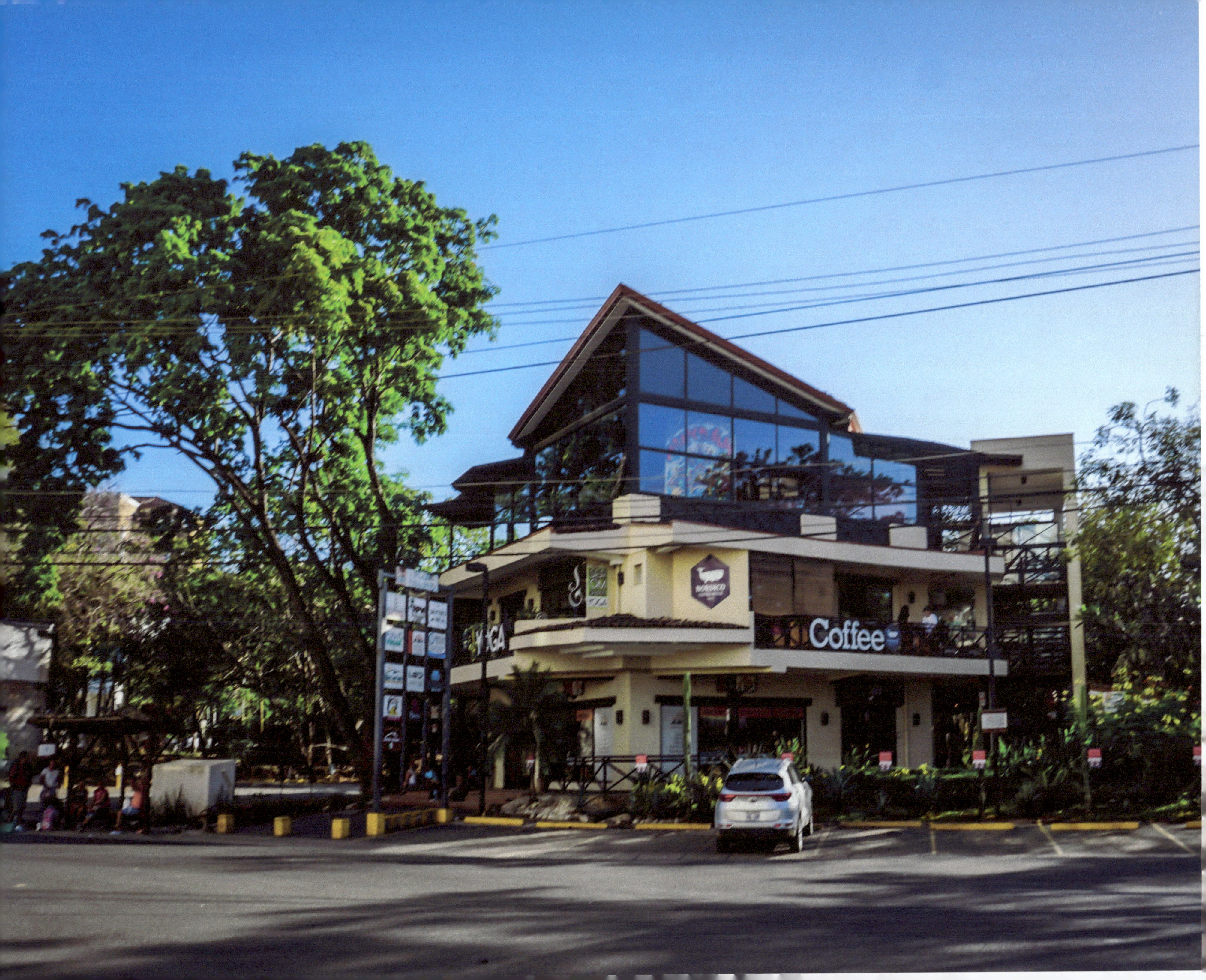
BOSSICO
Coffee

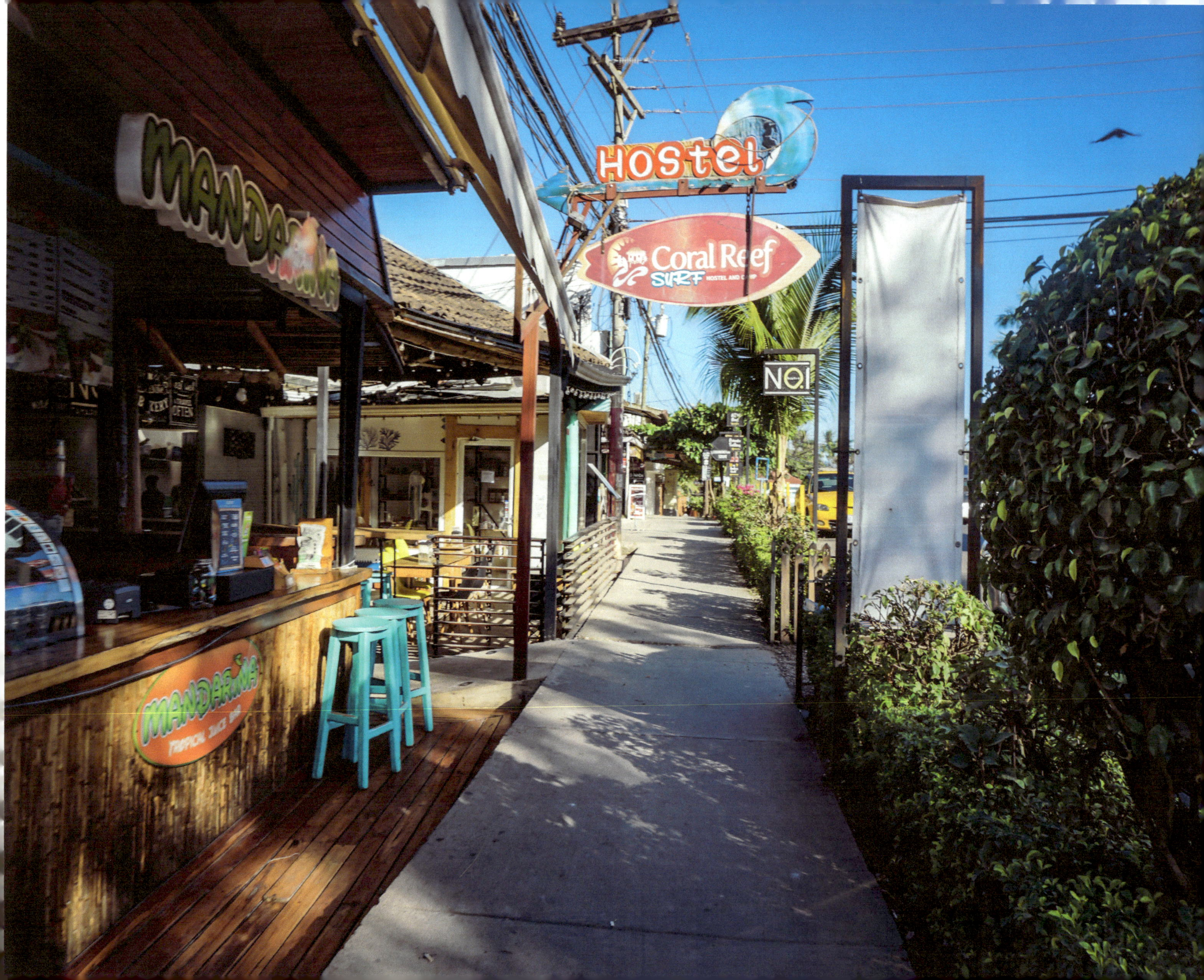

MANDARINA
Hostel
Coral Reef
SURF
HOSTEL AND CAMP
NO.1
MANDARINA
TROPICAL JUICE BAR

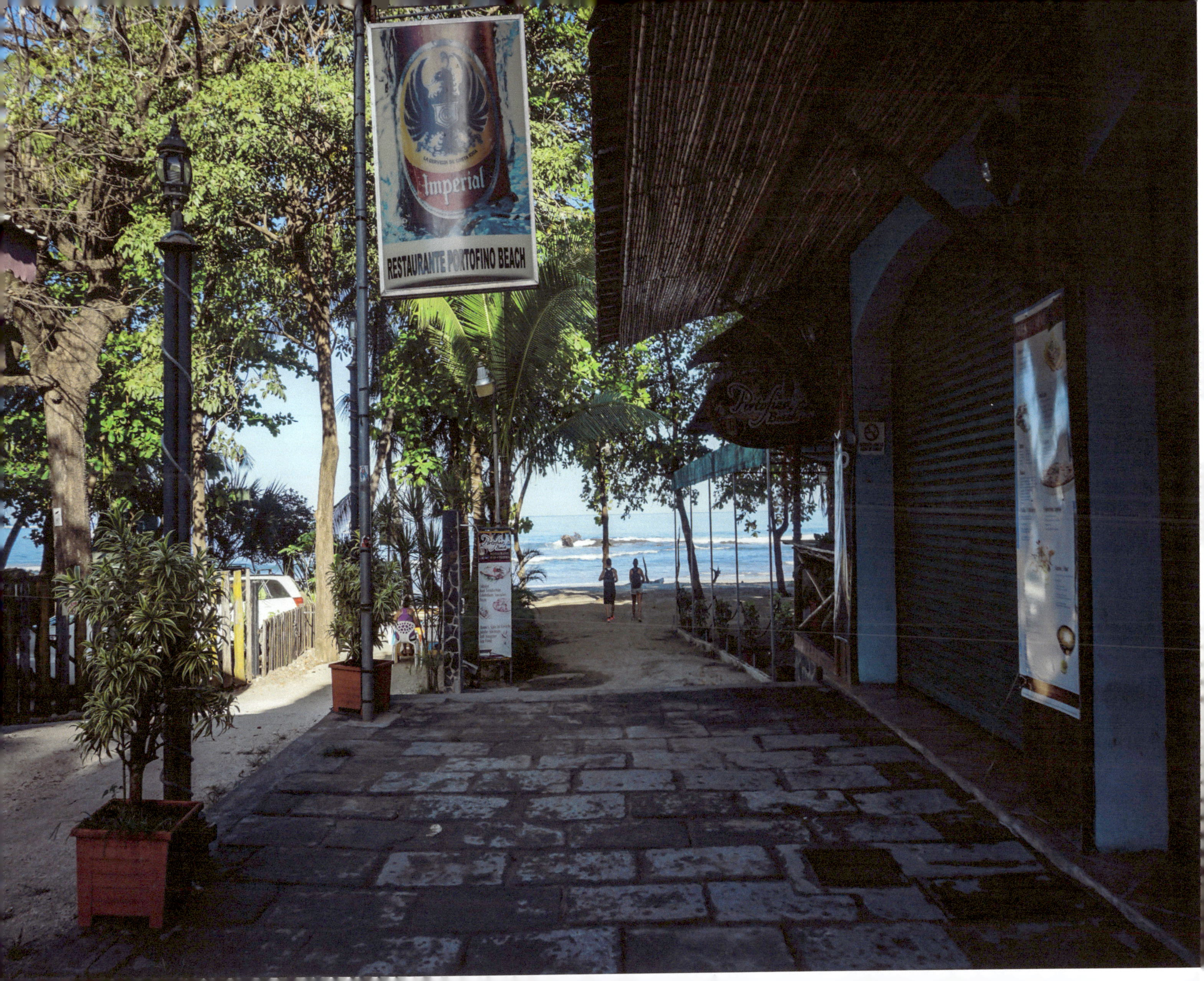

Imperial
RESTAURANTE PORTOFINO BEACH

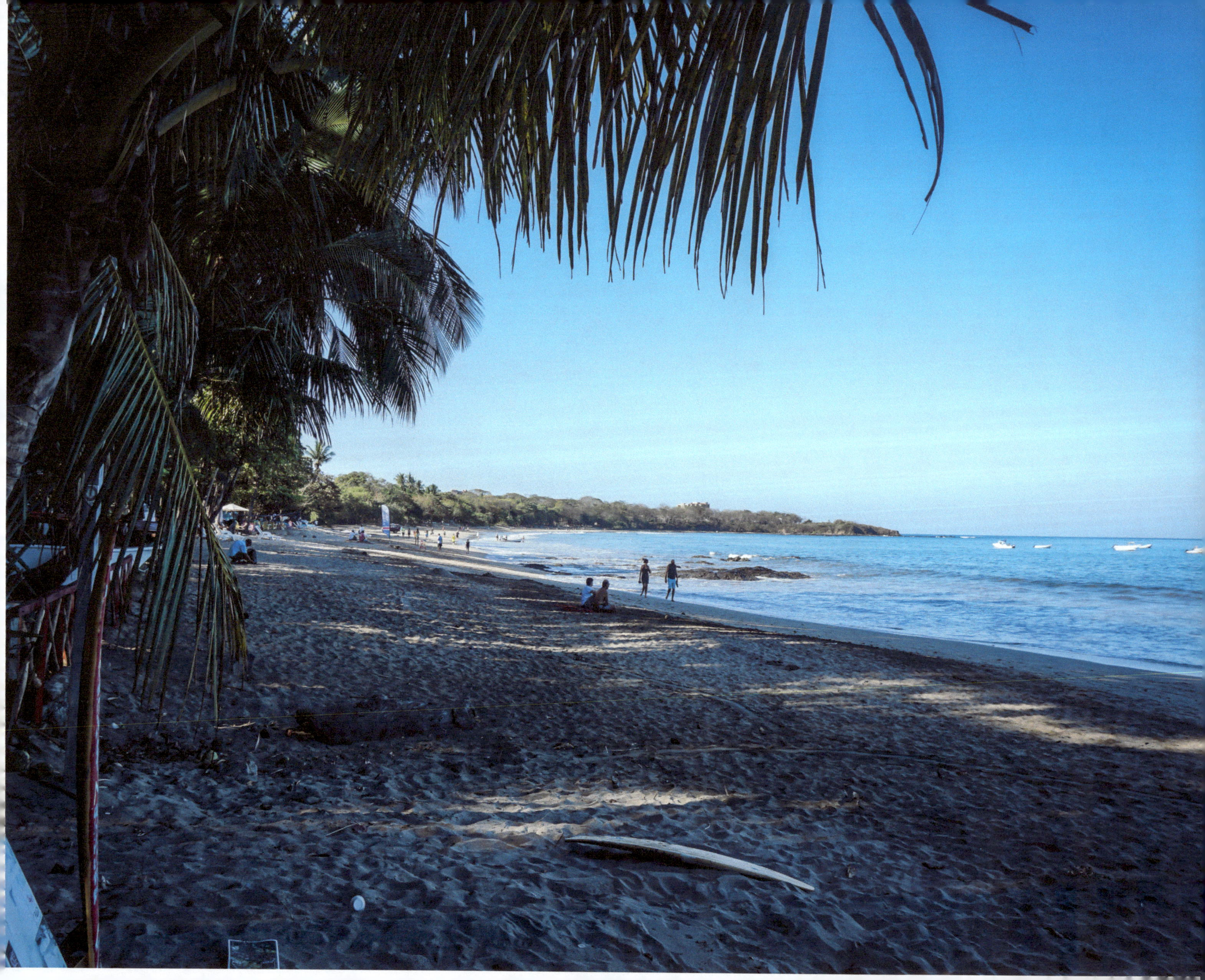

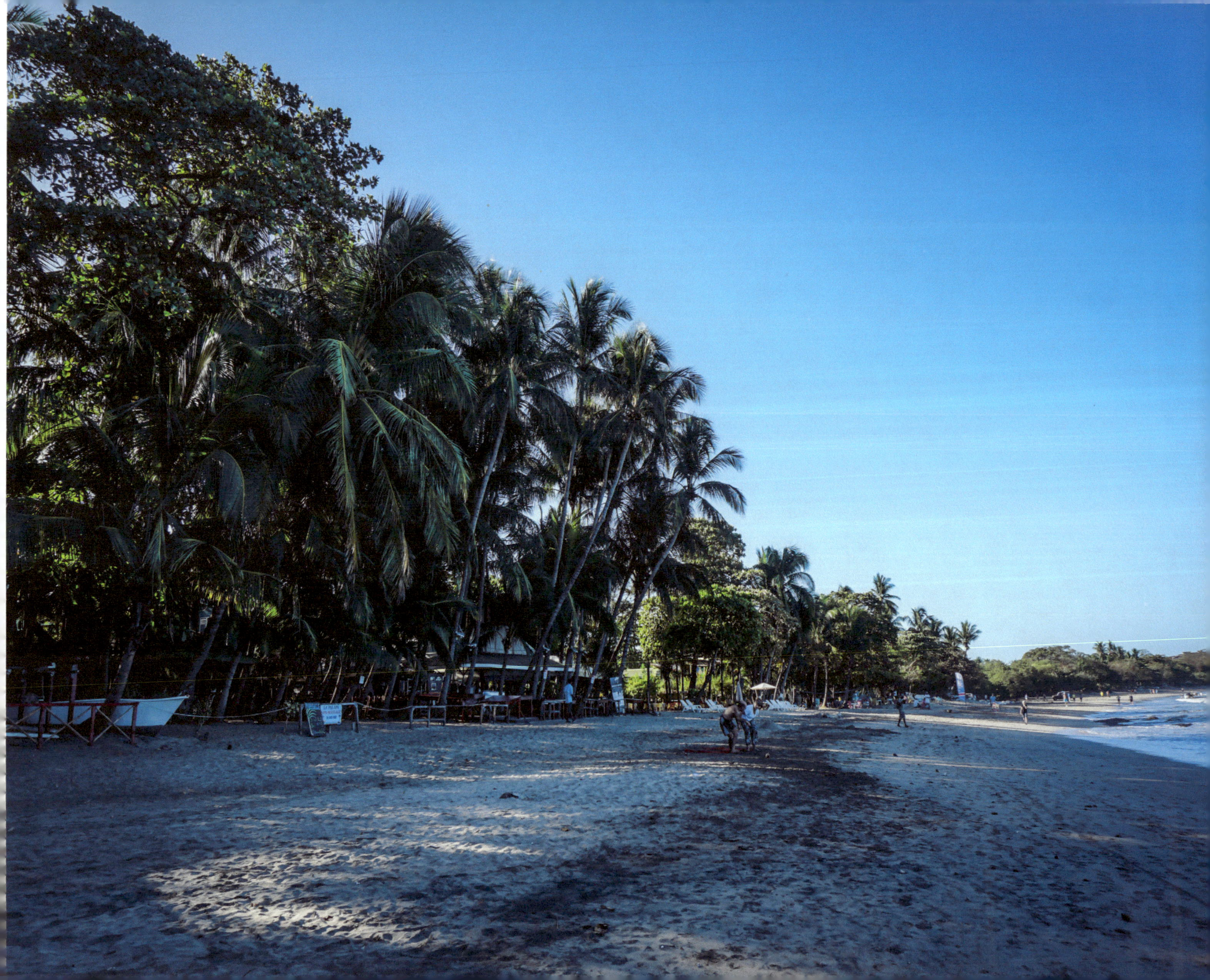

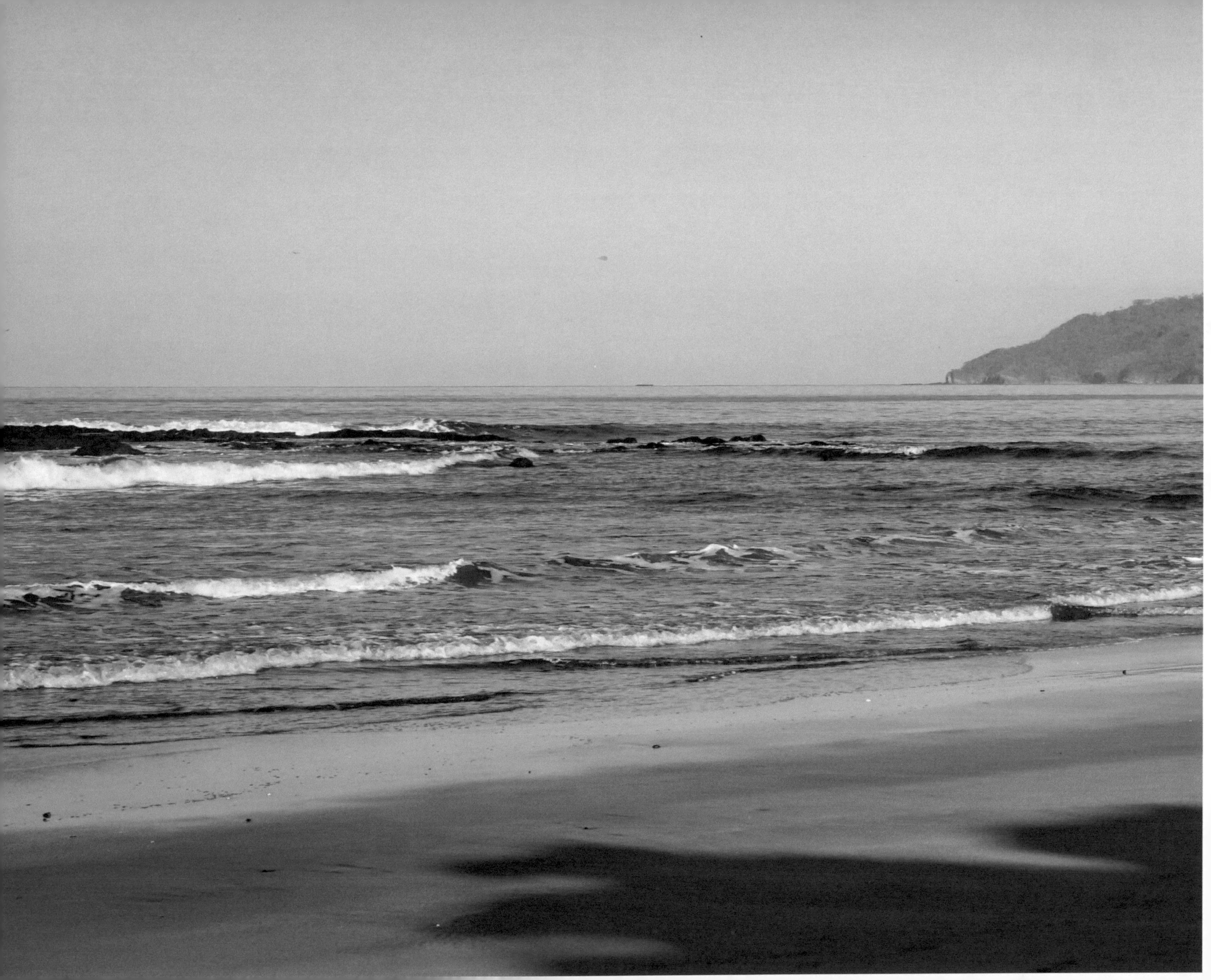

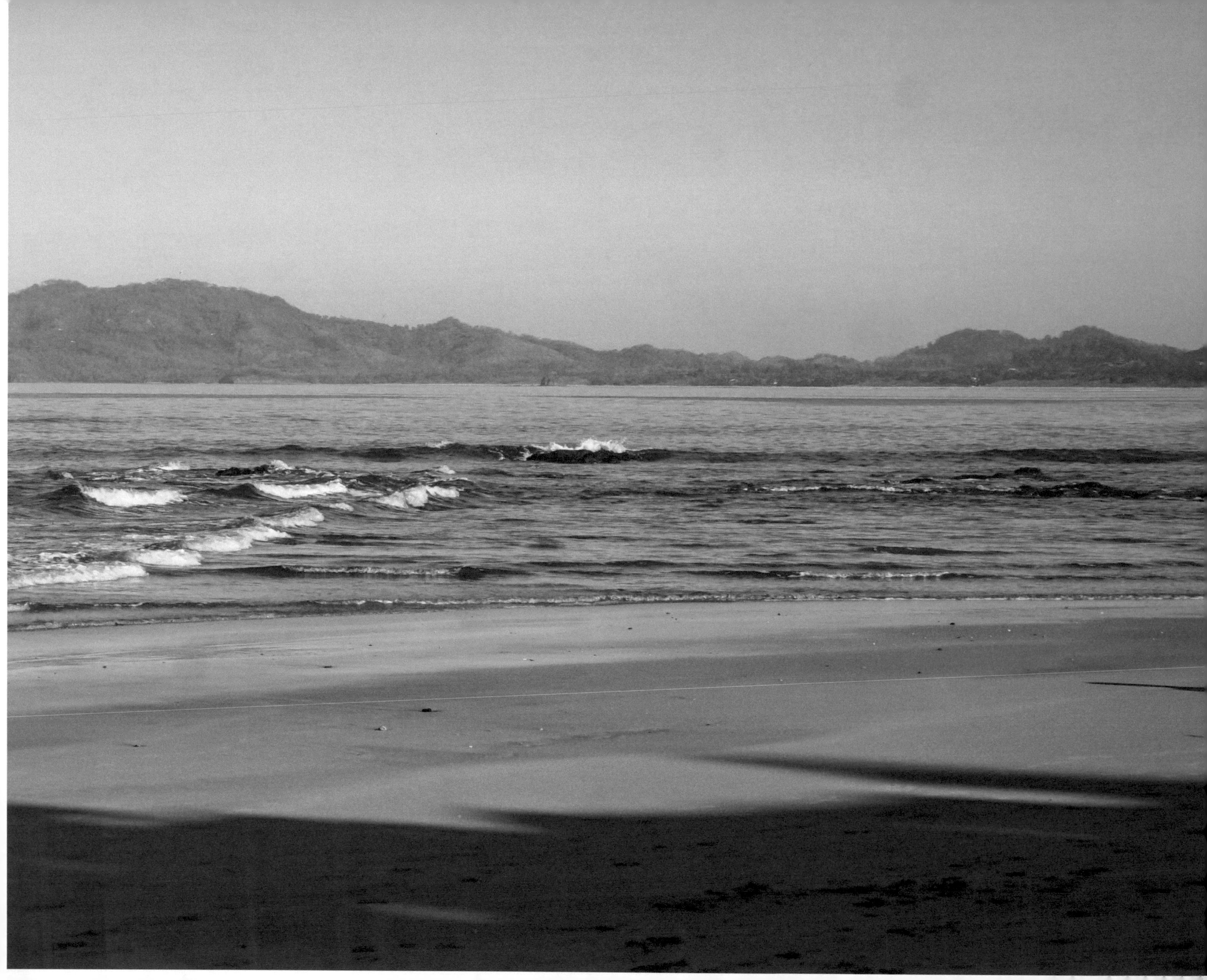

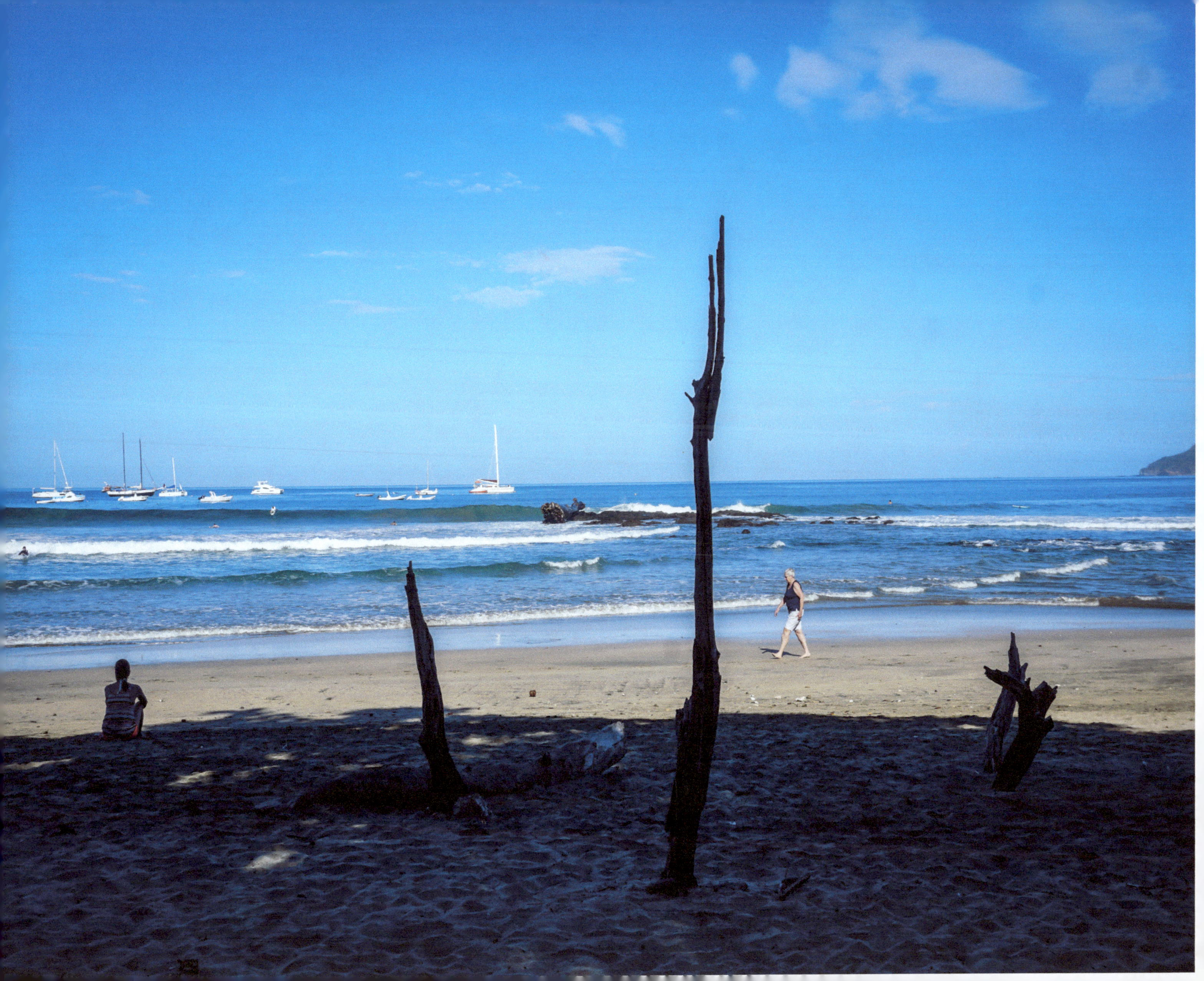

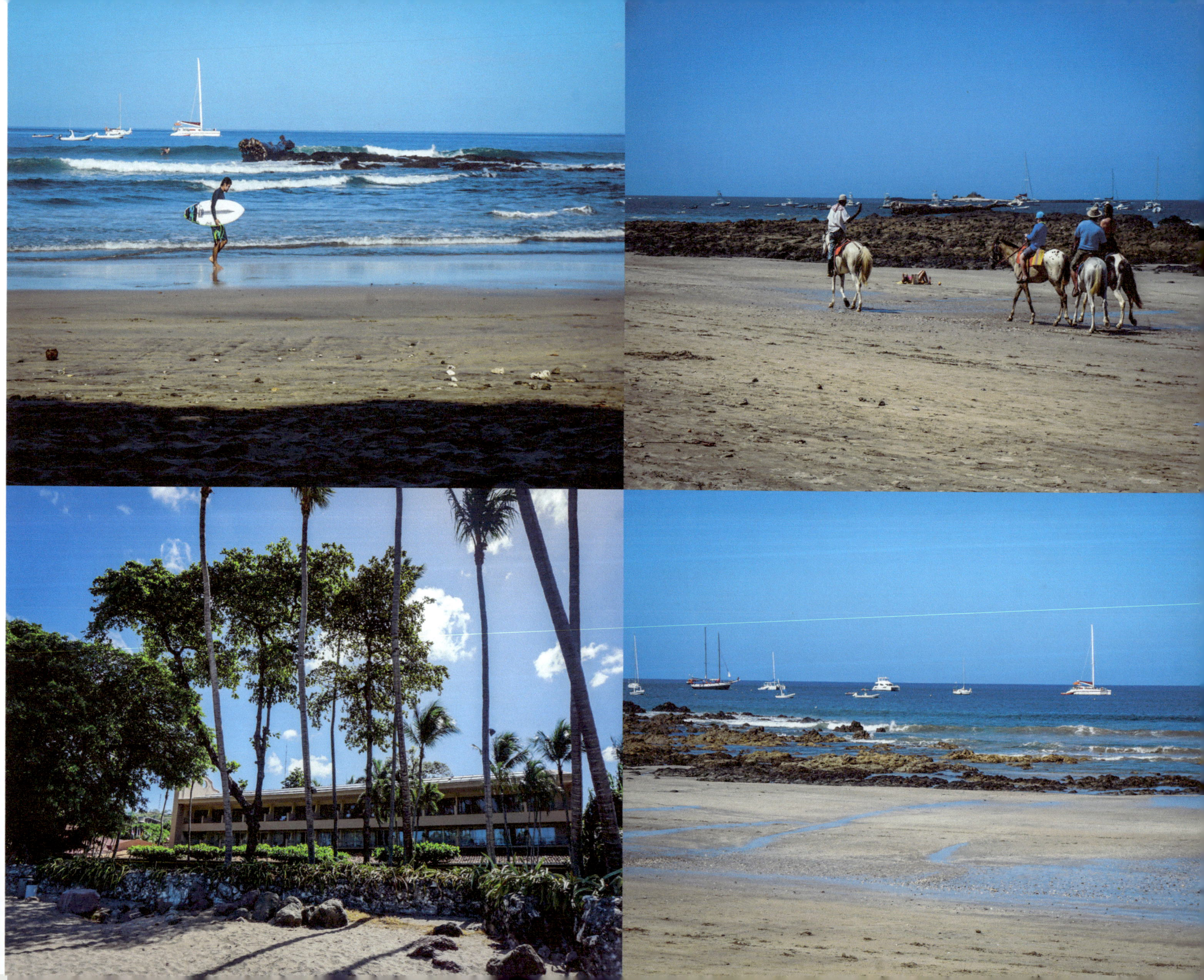

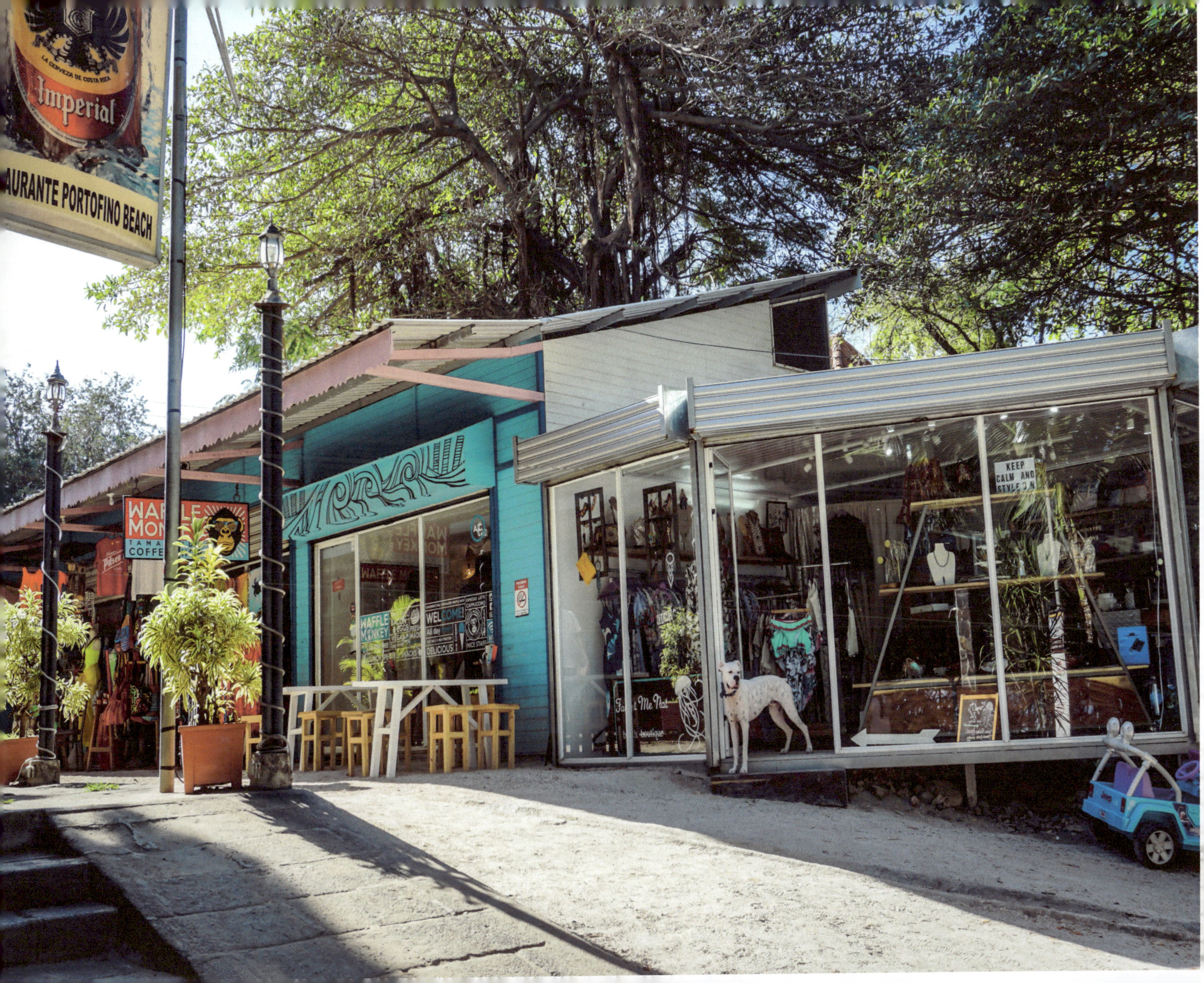
Imperial
LA CERVEZA DE COSTA RICA
AURANTE PORTOFINO BEACH
WAFFLE MONKEY
TAMA
COFFE
Pilsen
WAFFLE MONKEY
WELCOME!
All day
DELICIOUS!
NICE STABLE
KEEP
CALM AND
STYLE ON
Find Me Nat
boutique

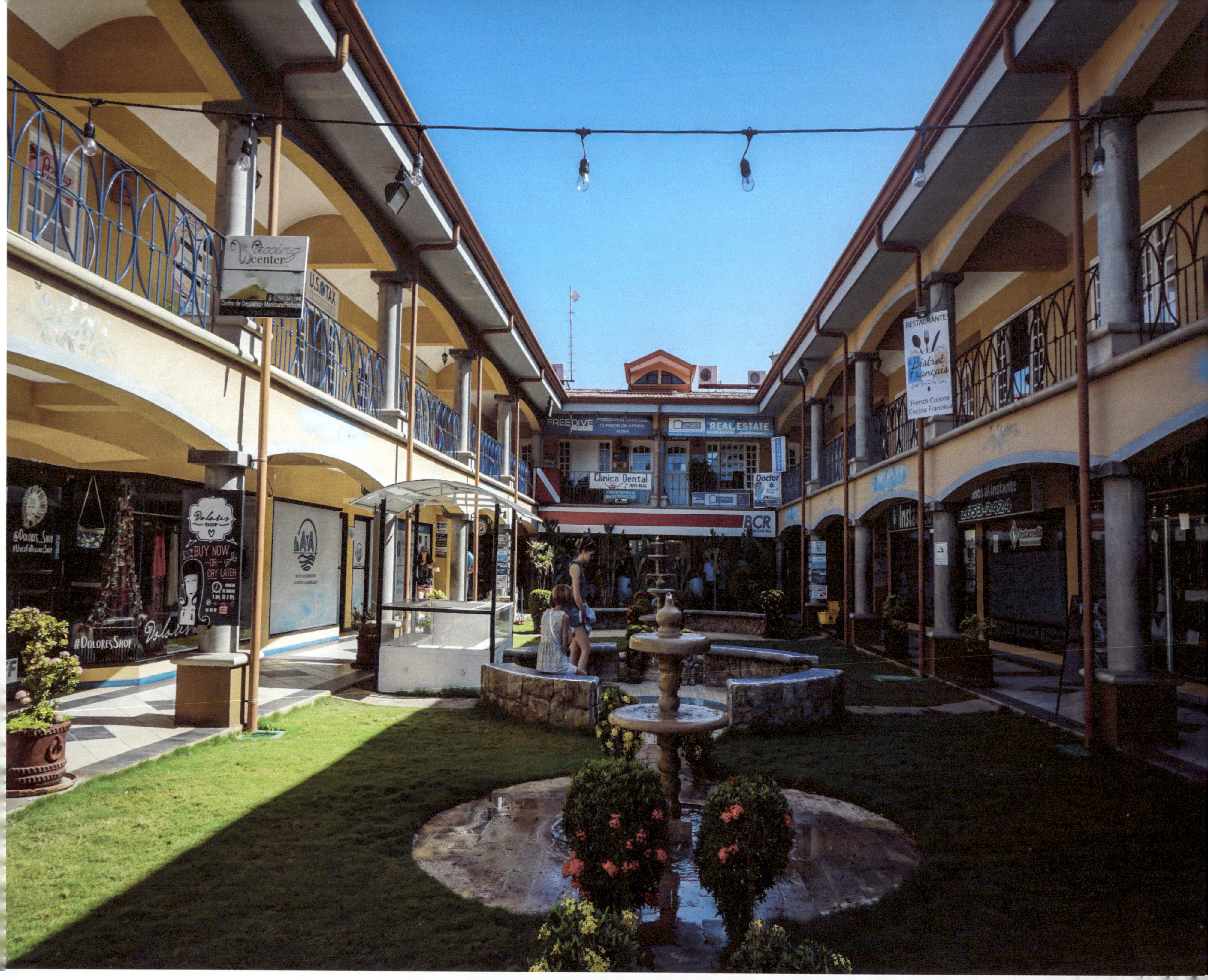
Boxing center
U.S. TAX
FREEDIVE
REAL ESTATE
Clinica Dental
Doctor
BCR
Dolores SHOP
BUY NOW
-OR-
CRY LATER
#DoloresShop
@Dolores_Shop
RESTAURANTE
Bistrot
Français
French Cuisine
Cocina Francesa

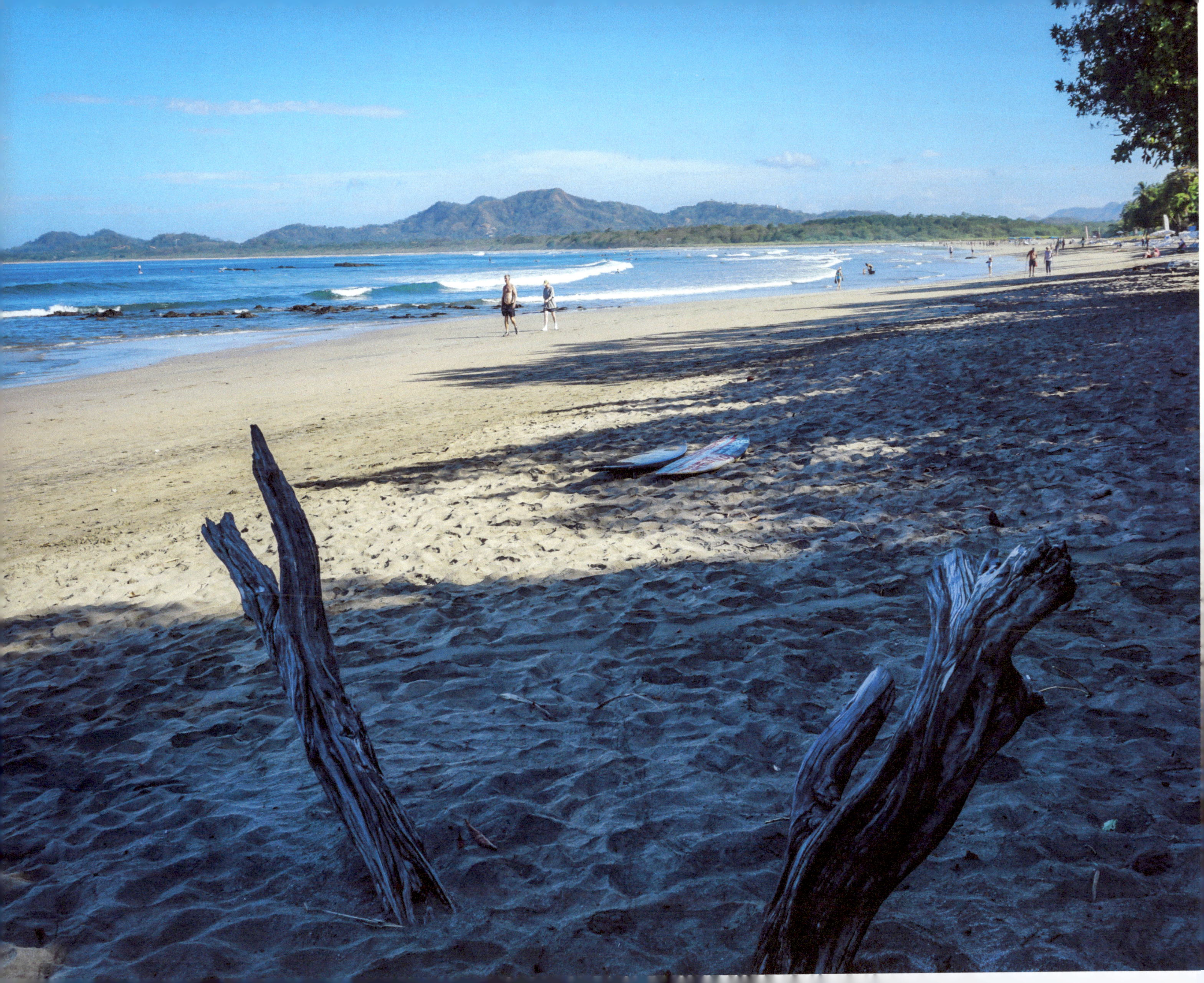

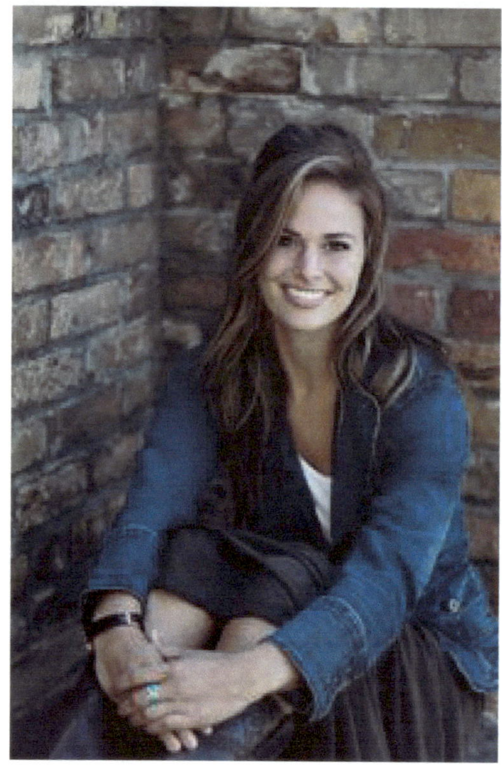

Social Media & Contact

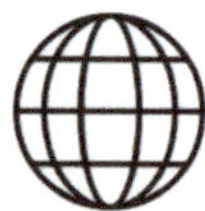 www.shutter-fotos.ca

 elyse@shutter-fotos.ca

 @shutter_fotos

 @ShutterFotos

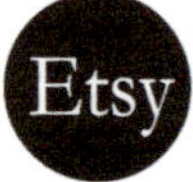 @FotoBoothphotography

About the Author

Elyse Booth is an international photographer and educator. She has travelled around the world photographing nature, people, culture, architectural icons, animals and lifestyle content. A few of the places she has travelled to include: Hawaii, Iceland, Thailand, Cambodia, Malaysia, Laos, Italy, France, Ireland, Croatia, Hungary, Czech Republic, England, Scotland, Costa Rica, Bermuda and Mexico.

Elyse is an award winning Google trusted photographer. She builds virtual tours for Google Maps through her business Shutter Fotos, www.shutter-fotos.ca. Elyse has been recognized as a top performer for Google and top five in North America for her tours.

Elyse has a passion for lifelong learning. In addition to her love for travel and photography, she teaches Communications Technology in the private and public educational systems.

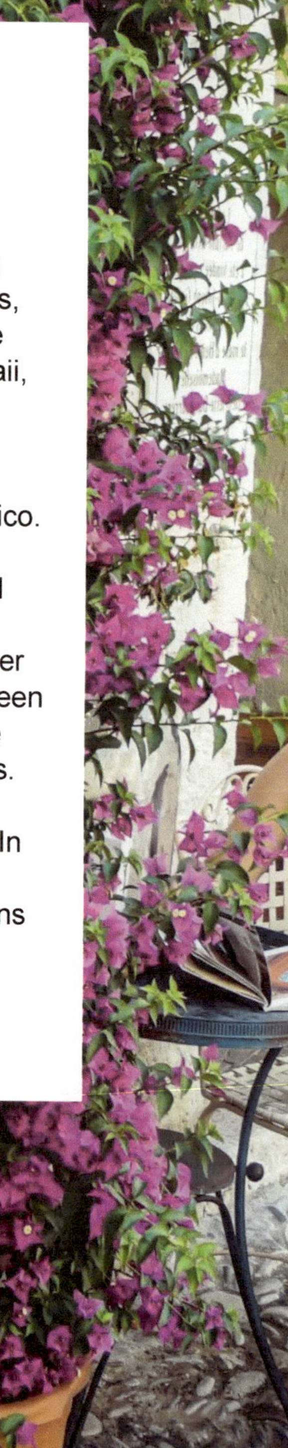

9 781990 241017